TWENTY-FIFTH ANNIVERSARY SERIES

2

Price-Quantity Interactions
in Business Cycles

PRICE-QUANTITY INTERACTIONS IN BUSINESS CYCLES

Frederick C. Mills
COLUMBIA UNIVERSITY

NATIONAL BUREAU OF ECONOMIC RESEARCH, INC.

NEW YORK, 1946

127152

Relation of the Directors to the Work and Publications
of the
National Bureau of Economic Research

1. The object of the National Bureau of Economic Research is to ascertain and to present to the public important economic facts and their interpretation in a scientific and impartial manner. The Board of Directors is charged with the responsibility of ensuring that the work of the Bureau is carried on in strict conformity with this object.

2. To this end the Board of Directors shall appoint one or more Directors of Research.

3. The Director or Directors of Research shall submit to the members of the Board, or to its Executive Committee, for their formal adoption, all specific proposals concerning researches to be instituted.

4. No report shall be published until the Director or Directors of Research shall have submitted to the Board a summary drawing attention to the character of the data and their utilization in the report, the nature and treatment of the problems involved, the main conclusions and such other information as in their opinion would serve to determine the suitability of the report for publication in accordance with the principles of the Bureau.

5. A copy of any manuscript proposed for publication shall also be submitted to each member of the Board. For each manuscript to be so submitted a special committee shall be appointed by the President, or at his designation by the Executive Director, consisting of three Directors selected as nearly as may be one from each general division of the Board. The names of the special manuscript committee shall be stated to each Director when the summary and report described in paragraph (4) are sent to him. It shall be the duty of each member of the committee to read the manuscript. If each member of the special committee signifies his approval within thirty days, the manuscript may be published. If each member of the special committee has not signified his approval within thirty days of the transmittal of the report and manuscript, the Director of Research shall then notify each member of the Board, requesting approval or disapproval of publication, and thirty additional days shall be granted for this purpose. The manuscript shall then not be published unless at least a majority of the entire Board and a two-thirds majority of those members of the Board who shall have voted on the proposal within the time fixed for the receipt of votes on the publication proposed shall have approved.

6. No manuscript may be published, though approved by each member of the special committee, until forty-five days have elapsed from the transmittal of the summary and report. The interval is allowed for the receipt of any memorandum of dissent or reservation, together with a brief statement of his reasons, that any member may wish to express; and such memorandum of dissent or reservation shall be published with the manuscript if he so desires. Publication does not, however, imply that each member of the Board has read the manuscript, or that either members of the Board in general, or of the special committee, have passed upon its validity in every detail.

7. A copy of this resolution shall, unless otherwise determined by the Board, be printed in each copy of every National Bureau book.

(Resolution adopted October 25, 1926 and revised February 6, 1933 and February 24, 1941)

Foreword

I am indebted to Wesley C. Mitchell, Arthur F. Burns, and Solomon Fabricant, my colleagues on the research staff of the National Bureau, for suggestions, criticisms and comments that have helped in the shaping of this study. Miss Martha Anderson has given valued editorial aid. H. Irving Forman has contributed his skill to the preparation of the charts. I am warmly appreciative of the friendly counsel and understanding aid given me by J. E. Morton during several summers of association with the National Bureau. Finally, I must record my deep obligations to Maude Remey Pech and Mildred G. Uhrbrock, my continuing helpers and my immediate associates in this enterprise.

FREDERICK C. MILLS

∢CONTENTS≻

◁LIST OF TABLES▷

LIST OF CHARTS

Price-Quantity Interactions
in Business Cycles

⊰CHAPTER 1⊱

INTRODUCTION: PHYSICAL VOLUME, UNIT PRICES, AND MONETARY VALUES IN BUSINESS CYCLES

THERE is a familiar distinction in economics between the physical or 'real' level of activities and the monetary level. At the one, we are concerned with the expenditure of physical energy and the use of physical materials in the production and distribution of goods. At the other, attention is given to the money values of commodities and services—values of individual goods, groups of commodities, or large aggregates. The continuing activities of economic life center on the stream of physical goods and services and on the flow of payments that is its monetary counterpart.

In the expansions and contractions of business cycles the flow of both goods and values are affected.[1] There are changes in the quantity of goods produced, of goods consumed, and of productive services rendered. There are, similarly, fluctuations in the aggregate values of goods and services—in the value of the national product, of consumers' outlay, of capital goods produced, and of commodities and services in various other categories. But the movements of the stream of goods and of the stream of values are not identical. Changing unit prices intervene, causing the two streams to fluctuate with different amplitudes and with different timings in their accelerations, their retardations, and their major changes of direction.

Thus, the cyclical movements of three related elements are of immediate interest to students of business cycles. Fluctuations in the number of physical units of goods produced and of services rendered interact with variations in unit prices to yield the expansions and contractions in value that are observable at the monetary level. Our purpose in this study is to obtain a better understanding of the relations among the cyclical fluctuations in values, prices, and quantities.

---

[1] Throughout this book the term 'value' is used to mean the monetary value of a commodity or group of commodities. In this sense value is the product of price per unit and number of physical units.

Such an understanding may be sought in two directions. One leads to study of the larger aggregates of values (aggregates built up from the monetary payments for individual commodities) and their price and quantity components. The most comprehensive form of such an aggregate would include total payments of all sorts in the economy—payments for goods at the raw materials stage, in semi-finished form, in finished form in wholesale and retail markets; wages and salaries; dividends, interest, and rent; taxes; payments of debts; payments for the transfer of title to real estate, securities, or other forms of property. In this form, of course, aggregate payments are many times[2] greater than the aggregate value of goods produced and services rendered. For total payments include much double counting of commodities, and are affected, also, by transfers of title that represent no change in physical form or properties. We deal in this report with a less inclusive aggregate, the value of goods currently produced and of services currently rendered. In the study of this aggregate (and its major components) one would ask: To what extent do expansions and contractions of business represent changes in the money value of spending and income, merely, and to what extent changes in the underlying stream of physical goods and services? How do the unit price and physical quantity factors interact? How do their amplitudes of change compare, their rates of expansion and contraction at different stages of cycles, their timing in cyclical movements?

The other direction leads to study of the relations between the prices and quantities of individual commodities, under the impact of cyclical forces. The essence of an enterprise economy lies in the interplay of prices and quantities, and in their mutual adaptation. Economists have pictured these adjustments as effected through shifting supply and demand relations, and have thought of these relations as definable in a tissue of supply and demand functions. Such functions, static in conception yet

[2] Some 10 or 11 times at least. Bank debits, as estimated by the Board of Governors of the Federal Reserve System, are approximately 10 times the gross national product, as estimated by Simon Kuznets. Cash payments would increase this ratio. A study of the flow of payments is now being conducted for the National Bureau of Economic Research by Morris Copeland.

subject to change over time in both shape and position, are inadequate instruments for the study of the price-quantity adjustments that occur as business cycles run their course. Only in imagination can dynamic changes be separated from static relations. For present purposes dynamic aspects are the central objects of investigation. We must do what we can to define and understand correlative cyclical changes in the prices and quantities of individual commodities and corresponding changes in the outlays of buyers.

In tracing these movements two problems concern us. We shall in the first place examine the interrelated movements of commodity prices and quantities during business cycles. Quantities produced, consumed, or traded constitute the physical bases of economic accomplishment, and of existence. Prices are the bases of exchange, the measures of relative worth, the keys to the allocation and utilization of resources. In some sectors of the economy individual producers and, indeed, whole industries effect adjustment to the forces of business cycles by modifying the physical quantities produced and marketed. In other sectors producers adjust to cyclical changes by altering unit prices.[3] In other words, business cycles, as they are manifest in certain sectors of the economy, are primarily quantity phenomena; in other sectors they are primarily price phenomena; in still other sectors the quantity and price factors dispute the primacy. The economic and social consequences of these two modes of accommodation are, of course, widely different. In seeking light on how prices and quantities interact in various markets during business cycles we shall be exploring these two modes of adaptation.

[3] It is convenient to speak of the 'adjustments' effected in business cycles through the price-quantity mechanism. The term doubtless implies that through related changes in the prices and quantities of individual commodities adaptation is effected, in commodity markets and in producing units, to external forces associated with cycles in the economy at large. This is not, I think, an inadmissible assumption. It is true, of course, that the price-quantity movements of each commodity influence, in their turn, other economic series, and that business cycles at large are composed of congeries of such interacting changes. The initiatory role of any one pair of price and quantity series in a business cycle is not great, however, so it is justifiable to think of cyclical movements in one pair of series as primarily 'adjustment effecting'.

The second problem has to do with outlay patterns for individual commodities. The total value of the output of a given commodity in a given period is computed by multiplying the number of units produced by the average unit price. This gives the required measure of the monetary outlays of buyers of that commodity (or of the revenues of sellers).[4] Having such measures for a substantial sample of commodities we may study, in detail, the ebbs and flows of buyers' outlays, for various classes of goods, and determine the relative roles of price and quantity changes in the cyclical fluctuations of monetary payments.

The present investigation is concerned primarily with the mechanism of price-quantity adjustments, for individual com-

[4] In deriving our measures of monetary outlay, or value, from unit price and quantity records it is assumed that goods changing hands in any given month have been sold at the prices quoted in that month. If the value measures are taken to represent a current flow of monetary payments, it is further assumed that payments are made at the time of the transfer of the physical goods. Obviously, neither assumption is strictly accurate. For some commodities contracts may be made well in advance of delivery, at prices that are constant for the season, regardless of the course of current quotations. Even without such contracts delivery may be made with a lag, i.e., current prices may relate to deliveries to be made weeks later.

The transfer of funds in settlement of a sale may, in turn, lag behind the transfer of the goods. Since we do not have the information concerning market practices that would be necessary to correct for such lags, we assume that price quotations, physical deliveries, and monetary payments are synchronous, within the time period set by the use of monthly data and by the process of averaging by cyclical stages (see App. Table 1). This averaging process irons out many of the time differences. The assumption that changes are synchronous, within the limits indicated, probably accords with the facts for many of the commodities here studied; for some it is clearly in error. In particular, for some commodities actual monetary flows doubtless lag behind the movements recorded for the present value series. These value series, in fact, may be regarded as indexes of the volume of financial commitments, on the part of buyers, rather than as measures of actual cash payments. It will be convenient, however, to use the term 'outlays of buyers', but the reservations here suggested should be borne in mind in the interpretation of results.

Similar reservations apply to the term 'revenues of sellers'. When freight charges, commissions, and other transfer payments are to be met by buyer or seller, sellers' receipts and buyers' outlays are not identical. However, since the broad cyclical swings of these two aggregates are closely parallel, I have used the terms interchangeably.

The present measures of monetary outlays are presented as first approximations to the cyclical fluctuations in the volume of monetary payments that parallel the transfer of physical goods. In a more accurate set of records account would be taken of the leads and lags that grow out of varying trade practices in the exchange of economic goods.

modities, and with outlay and revenue patterns for these commodities, separately and in various aggregative forms. We do not attempt to deal with total monetary payments in the economy at large. However, it will be helpful to introduce the discussion by a brief survey indicative of the character and dimensions of the value, price, and physical volume changes that have occurred in the United States during a recent period. In this, we utilize estimates of gross national product made by Simon Kuznets.[5]

Gross National Product, United States, 1919-1938

Av. annual value, millions of dollars	75,653
Av. change in 5 cyclical expansions	
Absolute, millions of dollars	+14,464
As percentage of av. annual value	+19.1
Av. change in 5 cyclical contractions	
Absolute, millions of dollars	−14,079
As percentage of av. annual value	−18.6

The fluctuations in gross national product, as averaged for these five cycles in general business, were substantial. In both expansions and contractions the average movement exceeded $14 billion. In relative terms, the annual accretions to gross national product during business expansions averaged 19.1 percent of the mean annual gross product; losses during contractions averaged 18.6 percent.[6] Losses have on the average almost equaled the gains of expansion. (Declines were exceptionally severe on the whole in the sample of recent cycles here included. Long-run American experience would show relatively greater gains in expansion.)

Do these cyclical fluctuations in the money value of gross national product represent equally large movements in the aggregate of goods and services that make up the *real* national product? What part do price changes play in the cyclical swings

---

[5] *National Product since 1869* (National Bureau of Economic Research, in press).

[6] The base is the average of the annual values. Measured against average values in years when cyclical lows were reached, the cyclical increments to gross national product average 20.0 percent. Declines during contraction average 16.2 percent of average values in peak years.

The observations on which these measures are based are annual aggregates. The cyclical fluctuations would be substantially larger if monthly figures were available.

of total value? Kuznets' materials help to answer these questions. His reports provide estimates of gross national product in 'constant' dollars. By the use of deflating indexes the effects of changing unit prices have been eliminated, so far as possible. From estimates expressed in 1929 dollars we derive measures of relative changes in gross national product during cyclical expansions and contractions. These we may take to define, with reasonable precision, changes in the physical quantities that underlie the value aggregate. These measures, with corresponding estimates of average changes in unit prices, are given in Table 1.

TABLE 1

Cyclical Changes in Estimated Annual Value and
Aggregate Physical Volume of Gross National Product, and in the
Average Unit Price of its Components, 1919-1938

AV. CHANGES IN 5 BUSINESS CYCLES, AS PERCENTAGES
OF AV. ANNUAL FIGURES

	Expansion	Contraction	Full Cycle Amplitude [a]
Aggregate value	+19.1	—18.6	+37.7
Aggregate physical volume	+15.2	—9.1	+24.3
Average unit price	+3.4	—10.5	+13.9

[a] Algebraic difference between the change in expansion and the change in contraction.

During the five business cycles between 1919 and 1938 swelling physical volume was the major factor in the expansions of the value of gross national product. The contribution of rising unit prices (which advanced, on the average, some 3 percent of their mean value) was not negligible, but it was distinctly less important than the increase in the number of physical units entering into the national product. In contractions the story is different. An average decline of 9.1 percent in the quantity factor was paralleled by a decline of 10.5 percent in unit prices. During this period cyclical fluctuations in the value of gross national product were dominated in expansions by increases in physical quantities; in contractions they were dominated, but by a much narrower margin, by declining unit prices. In the aggregate of movements in expansions and contractions the fluctuations of values exceeded those of the two components.

Quantity variations stood next, with a range of fluctuation substantially wider than that of prices.[7]

This general record deals with a short period. We cannot be sure that study of a longer period would yield the same results. (In a time of rising price trends, for example, relative price behavior in expansion and contraction phases would be different.) Moreover, there are cross-currents and differences that are not revealed by an aggregate as comprehensive as gross national product. For a more detailed picture of the interaction of prices and quantities and of the behavior of buyers' outlays during business cycles we turn to price quotations and corresponding quantity records for a selected sample of individual commodities. Building on basic measures derived by the business cycles staff of the National Bureau in its description of cyclical behavior,[8] we employ various methods that help to bring out the characteristics of outlay patterns and of related price and quantity movements. A brief account of the essential points needed for an understanding of our argument follows.

[7] The entries in the last column are not accurate measurements of cyclical amplitude, being derived from annual series fitted into the framework of general business cycles. See *Measuring Business Cycles*, Arthur F. Burns and Wesley C. Mitchell (National Bureau of Economic Research, 1946), Ch. 6, for a discussion of this point.

[8] For a detailed account of these methods of measurement see Burns and Mitchell, *op. cit.*

CHAPTER 2

METHODS OF DESCRIPTION AND ANALYSIS

Price-Quantity Changes in Business Cycles

ALL the measures here employed are based on 'reference cycle relatives', which define the average standing of each economic series at each of nine stages of business cycles. Stage I is the initial trough, stage V the peak, and stage IX the terminal trough; stages II, III, and IV mark off successive thirds of the phase of expansion in reference cycles, and stages VI, VII, and VIII mark off successive thirds of contraction. The turning points in general business activity defined by stages I, V, and IX are determined on the basis of extensive study of statistical records of economic processes of all sorts, supplemented by examination of contemporary appraisals of the state of business by financial writers, economists, and other students of business conditions.[1] The 'reference cycles' thus established provide a standard framework into which each of the many economic series to be studied is fitted. The original monthly data making up a given series, after correction for seasonal fluctuations (if these are present), are broken into segments, each covering a reference cycle.[2] The monthly entries making up a given segment are then expressed as percentages of their average for that reference cycle. Thus for the business cycle that extends from the trough of March 1933 through the peak of May 1937, to the

[1] The troughs and peaks of successive business cycles in the United States, over the period covered by the most extensive of the commodity records used in this study, are given below.

Trough		Peak		Trough		Trough		Peak		Trough	
Dec.	1858	Oct.	1860	June	1861	Dec.	1900	Sep.	1902	Aug.	1904
June	1861	Apr.	1865	Dec.	1867	Aug.	1904	May	1907	June	1908
Dec.	1867	June	1869	Dec.	1870	June	1908	Jan.	1910	Jan.	1912
Dec.	1870	Oct.	1873	Mar.	1879	Jan.	1912	Jan.	1913	Dec.	1914
Mar.	1879	Mar.	1882	May	1885	Dec.	1914	Aug.	1918	Apr.	1919
May	1885	Mar.	1887	Apr.	1888	Apr.	1919	Jan.	1920	Sep.	1921
Apr.	1888	July	1890	May	1891	Sep.	1921	May	1923	July	1924
May	1891	Jan.	1893	June	1894	July	1924	Oct.	1926	Dec.	1927
June	1894	Dec.	1895	June	1897	Dec.	1927	June	1929	Mar.	1933
June	1897	June	1899	Dec.	1900	Mar.	1933	May	1937	May	1938

[2] Appropriately modified procedures are used for annual and quarterly data.

terminal trough of May 1938, the average monthly amount of merchant pig iron produced was 317,000 tons. (This is an average of seasonally corrected monthly entries.) Production in March 1933 (seasonally corrected) was 75,000 tons. The March reference cycle relative is 100 x (75,000/317,000), or 24. A similar figure is computed for each of the other months between March 1933 and May 1938. These reference cycle relatives, averaged by reference cycle stages, constitute the materials of the present investigation.

The special methods and measurements used in this study may be exemplified with reference to the price of pig iron and the quantity and value of merchant pig iron produced in the United States during the nine business cycles that ran their course between August 1904 and May 1938. Stage averages of reference cycle relatives, computed from monthly measurements for these nine cycles, are given in Table 2, for these series. The three patterns are shown graphically in Chart 1.

TABLE 2

Average Movements of Unit Price, Physical Volume,
and Aggregate Value of Merchant Pig Iron Produced
Nine Business Cycles, 1904-1938

STAGE MEASURES

Reference Cycle Stages

	I	II	III	IV	V	VI	VII	VIII	IX
Price	85	88	97	112	118	114	105	94	90
Quantity	73	86	102	120	133	132	106	76	65
Value	63	75	95	130	151	145	109	72	59

	PHASE MEASURES, AVERAGE CHANGE		FULL CYCLE MEASURE
	Expansion	Contraction	Average Amplitude
Price	+33	—28	+ 61
Quantity	+60	—68	+128
Value	+88	—92	+180

The average patterns of pig iron prices and the value of merchant production show advances between reference stages I and V, and declines between stages V and IX. These movements of the averages accord perfectly with the expansions and recessions of business cycles. Merchant production behaves similarly, except that it remains virtually stable between stages V and VI.

CHART 1

Pig Iron: Average Movements of Unit Price, Merchant Production, and Aggregate Value of Merchant Production
Nine Business Cycles, 1904–1938

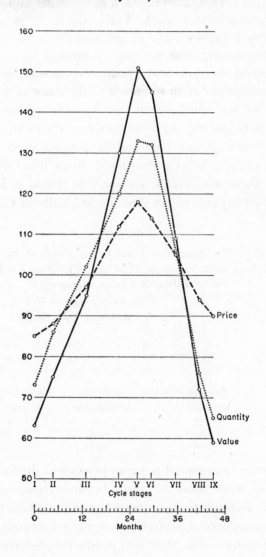

Thereafter it drops more sharply than prices. The three patterns differ notably in the amplitudes of cyclical swings (Table 2). In terms of the indexes there given the amplitude of fluctuations in quantity is approximately twice that of the fluctuations in price,[3] and the amplitude of fluctuations in value is approximately three times that of fluctuations in price.

Relatives defining the average standing at nine reference cycle stages of comparable price and quantity series, treated as coordinate observations on related variables, are admirably adapted to the study of the cyclical adjustments effected through the price-quantity mechanism. The procedures here employed make possible the massing of evidence relating to concurrent shifts in market prices and in quantities produced (or sold, or consumed) during expansion and contraction phases of business cycles. These procedures are briefly described and explained.

Correlative cyclical changes in prices and in quantities may be graphically portrayed by superimposing the average patterns of reference cycle changes in these factors. Pig iron prices and merchant pig iron production illustrate the procedure (Chart 1). A common framework (defined by the dates of initial trough, peak, terminal trough, and intervening stages) has been imposed on the price and production series, for each of the nine reference cycles covered. The relatives for the two series are thus comparable in respect of the time factor. As we have seen, the production series is marked on the average by wider amplitude of cyclical swings, sharper advance in the early stages of expansion, and tardier but more violent response to the forces

[3] In this and subsequent tables the 'war cycles' are included. ('War cycles' are here defined as those occurring between 1861 and 1867, and between 1914 and 1921.) Since these cycles were marked by exceptionally violent price fluctuations, the effect of their inclusion is to give price amplitude averages greater than those that would be obtained from peacetime performance alone. The degree to which certain of our basic measures are modified by the exclusion of data for war cycles is indicated at various points in the following account, but our present concern is with the inclusive record.

In comparing price and quantity amplitudes for pig iron and certain other commodities we must bear in mind that some part of the total output may change hands at the peak of prosperity at prices above those currently quoted in trade papers, and that at the lowest point of depression some part of the output may be sold at prices below current quotations. The resulting bias may be wholly or partly offset by sales on long-term contracts, at prices much more stable than those currently quoted.

of recession. These movements can be traced with precision, and in detail, on the superimposed graphs.

A different and in some respects more illuminating representation of the correlated movements of prices and quantities during business cycles is obtained when the average reference cycle relatives of the price and production series are plotted as coordinates (Chart 2, Fig. 1). The point marking the average standing of prices and production at reference cycle stage I is defined by the abscissa 73 (production) and the ordinate 85

CHART 2

Patterns of Related Price-Quantity Movements in Business Cycles
Three Commodities
Averages by Cycle Stages

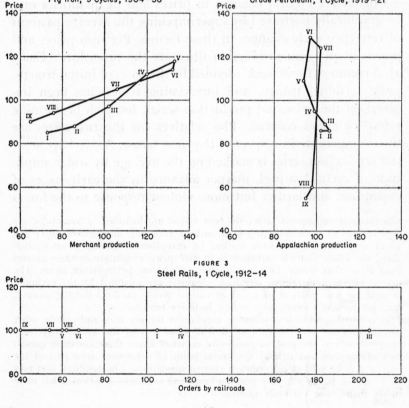

FIGURE 1
Pig Iron, 9 Cycles, 1904–38

FIGURE 2
Crude Petroleum, 1 Cycle, 1919–21

FIGURE 3
Steel Rails, 1 Cycle, 1912–14

(price). Similar points define the standings of the two variables at the other cyclical stages. The full pattern of concurrent price and production movements, as averaged for nine reference cycles, is traced on the diagram.[4]

This mode of presentation is effective in conveying the impression of coordinated changes in prices and production, during expansion and contraction phases of business cycles, and in indicating the relative importance of changes in each, in the various cyclical stages. Consideration of the forms this 'price-quantity pattern' would take under different conditions will make the meaning of a given type of pattern clearer. Thus if, for a given commodity, prices were the sole active factor in business cycles, with production stable, the diagram would take the form of a vertical line. An approach to this situation is represented by Chart 2, Fig. 2, showing correlated changes in the average price and production of crude petroleum in the Appalachian field from stage to stage of the business cycle that ran its course between April 1919 and September 1921. In the reverse case, when all cyclical adjustments are effected through quantity changes, prices remaining stable, the pattern would appear as a horizontal line. The price-production pattern for steel rails during the 1912-14 reference cycle exemplifies perfectly this type of behavior (Chart 2, Fig. 3). With equal changes in the two variables (i.e., equal in terms of reference cycle relatives), and with similar vertical and horizontal scales, the plotted points marking the standing of price and quantity components at reference cycle stages would all fall on a straight line inclined at 45 degrees to the horizontal. Chart 2, Fig. 1, roughly approximates this condition, though the inclination is somewhat less than 45 degrees because fluctuations in merchant pig iron production are greater than those in price. The inclination of such a diagram as a whole, it is clear, provides an indication of the relative roles of price and quantity changes in the ad-

[4] For a somewhat similar presentation, based on logarithms of annual production figures and of average annual prices, see W. W. Leontief, Price-Quantity Variations in Business Cycles, *Review of Economic Statistics*, May 1935. Leontief's study embodies the first formal work of this sort with which I am familiar. Our procedures were developed independently of Leontief's, but in the application of these methods we have benefited from Leontief's suggestive and original work.

justments that accompany business cycles. Moreover, the slopes of the lines connecting pairs of points in the diagram may be interpreted in the same way, with reference to changes between any two cyclical stages.

Joint Cyclical Variability and Its Components

A measure of cyclical amplitude was described in a preceding paragraph. In the study of joint variability an index of combined amplitude is needed—a measure of the amplitude of the movements of the price-quantity points that define the pattern of price-quantity behavior in reference cycles. Such a measure is given in Table 3, col. 2. The method employed may be ex-

TABLE 3

Joint Variability of Prices and Output of Merchant Pig Iron
Nine Business Cycles, 1904-1938

		PERCENTAGE	CONTRIBUTION	TO	JOINT	VARIABILITY			
	JOINT	Full Cycle		Expansion			Contraction		
	VARIABILITY	p	q	p	q	p+q	p	q	p+q
(1)	(2)	(3)	(4)	(5)	(6)	(7)	(8)	(9)	(10)
Av. reference cycle pattern	6,477	19	81	11	29	40	8	52	60

plained with reference to the figure 6,477, defining the joint variability of pig iron prices and merchant pig iron production in the average reference cycle pattern plotted in Chart 2, Fig. 1. This is a measure of the combined variability of the price and quantity factors about the point of averages of the pattern there shown. Thus for the nine points in Chart 2, Fig. 1, the point of averages is defined by the coordinates 99, 100 (i.e., 99 on the quantity axis, 100 on the price axis).[5] The point for stage I has the coordinates 73, 85. The deviation of point I from the point of averages is −26 on the x-axis, −15 on the y-axis; the sum of the squares of these two figures is 901. A similar figure may be computed for each of the other eight points marking out the average pattern of price-quantity behavior in reference cycles.

[5] These are the unweighted averages of the coordinates for the nine reference cycle stages. Were each stage measurement weighted according to the number of months represented by it—an unnecessary refinement for the present purpose—the averages of the coordinates for prices and quantities would be exactly 100, 100.

The total of the nine figures, equally weighted, is 6,477. This sum measures the magnitude of the pattern, or the amplitude of joint price-quantity movements in business cycles. It takes on significance, of course, when used for comparison of different commodities, or for studying chronological changes in the pattern of price-quantity behavior for a single commodity.

The measure of joint variability is composed of two elements —a series of price components and a series of quantity components. Thus, for the average reference cycle pattern, the sum of the price components (the squared y-deviations) for the nine points in Chart 2, Fig. 1, is 1,203; the sum of the quantity components (the squared x-deviations) for the same nine points is 5,274. As percentages of the total joint variability (6,477) these are, respectively, 19 and 81 (Table 3, col. 3 and 4). They indicate that, on the average, for merchant pig iron, price contributed 19 percent of the joint cyclical variability of prices and quantities; production contributed 81 percent.[6] These percentages provide valuable indications of the relative importance of price and quantity fluctuations in the cyclical adjustments effected through the price-quantity mechanism.

The total amplitude of movements in the prices and output of merchant pig iron, as manifest in the average reference cycle pattern, may be broken into components of another sort. The entries in Table 3, col. 7 and 10, indicate that 40 percent of the combined movements occur during the expansion phase of reference cycles, 60 percent during contraction.[7] This means

[6] The difference between these two figures is materially greater than that between the amplitude measures (61 for price, 128 for quantity) given in Table 2. The measures of joint variability take account of the positions of nine points, not merely of the low and high values. They are derived, moreover, from squared deviations. (The use of squared measurements is necessary for consistency among the components of the total variability.)

In the calculation of percentages for prices and quantities (19 and 81) no account is taken of the technical 'interaction' between the price and quantity components resulting from possible correlation between their cyclical movements. The present measures relate to the joint cyclical variability of prices and quantities when their separate variations are combined in the manner indicated. There is no analysis of variance (of pig iron values) in the technical sense.

[7] In this computation entries for stages I to V, inclusive, are considered to define the expansion phase; entries for stages V to IX are taken to define the contraction phase. The squared deviation for stage V is divided equally between the expansion and contraction phases.

that the combined deviations of price and quantity from their average cyclical standings are greater during business contractions than during business expansions. The impact of contraction on the price-quantity mechanism, for merchant pig iron, is heavier than that of expansion in the sense that joint price-quantity variability is greater during contraction. Further analysis shows that the 40 percent figure for expansion was composed of an 11 percent price contribution and a 29 percent production contribution, while the 60 percent figure for contraction was composed of an 8 percent price and a 52 percent production contribution (all these are percentages of the total joint variability of the average reference cycle pattern). Price is the smaller component during both expansion and recession. The deviations of pig iron prices from their cyclical average are wider and more sustained during reference expansion than during contraction; the reverse is true of merchant pig iron production, and in substantially greater degree.

Elasticity of Quantities and Flexibility of Prices in Business Cycles

The coordinate presentation of price and quantity changes, as in Chart 2, Fig. 1, suggests immediately the use of the customary measures of elasticity and flexibility.[8] Conceptually, coefficients of elasticity and flexibility are derived from equations of price-quantity relationships that are inverse and essentially timeless. Implicit in them is an assumption of causality. If the reference is to elasticity, quantities demanded are assumed to change because unit prices change; if the reference is to flexibility, prices

---

[8] The coefficient of elasticity of demand is given by the expression $\eta = y/x \cdot dx/dy$, where x is quantity and y is price. This coefficient is the ratio of a relative change in quantity (usually quantity demanded) to the corresponding relative change in unit price, the relative changes being infinitesimal. The quantity factor is the dependent variable. A given coefficient is assumed to relate to a moment of time or to a period within which tastes, income distribution, and other circumstances affecting individual demand schedules may be treated as fixed.

The coefficient of flexibility of price as given by Henry L. Moore is defined by the expression $\phi = x/y \cdot dy/dx$. This is the ratio of a relative change in price per unit of commodity to the corresponding relative change in quantity, the relative changes being infinitesimal. Unit price is here assumed to be the dependent variable.

are assumed to change because larger or smaller quantities are placed upon the market. It is conventional to speak of demand as elastic if η is greater than 1, inelastic if it is less than 1, and to speak of price as flexible if ϕ is greater than 1, inflexible if ϕ is less than 1.

When we follow the associated movements of prices and quantities in the framework of reference cycles we are dealing, obviously, with relations in the dimension of time, not with the relations assumed in the conventional diagrams. From one stage to another of business cycles we have a complex of changes in the many circumstances that affect individual and group demand schedules. With reference to the Cournot-Marshall diagrams, price movements from stage to stage of business cycles may reflect changes in the shape and location of demand curves, as well as movements along demand curves (interacting, of course, with similarly complex changes on the supply side). It is such changes as these that lie back of the shifts represented in the diagrams of Chart 2. Although the changes affecting quantity and price are due to diverse influences, there is reason to expect some orderliness in the behavior of the factors concerned, when studied in the framework of reference cycles, and there is justification for a systematic attempt to define these changes. Procedures deriving from those used by Cournot and Marshall may be employed, with frank recognition that we are dealing with changes in the dimension of time and that the resulting shifts reflect the play of varied dynamic forces in addition to movements along timeless curves of demand and supply. In the choice of symbols to define the resulting coefficients and of terms to describe price and quantity behavior, care should be taken to avoid confusion with the conventional meanings.

For the purposes of this study we shall use the term *elasticity*, but with qualifying adjectives or adjectival nouns to indicate the temporal reference. Thus we may speak of *stage elasticity* when we are referring to the relative responsiveness of physical quantity to price changes and to other economic forces acting between any two cyclical stages.[9] We may speak of *phase*

---

[9] The term 'responsiveness' is subject to qualifications similar to those that attach to 'adjustments' (see Ch. 1, note 3). Its use suggests that physical volume

elasticity when the reference is to responsiveness of quantity to price changes and to general economic forces (cyclical and other) during cyclical phases of expansion or contraction. We may speak of *full cycle elasticity* when an average of measurements for the phases of expansion and contraction is in question.[10] Other appropriate terms may be used when the behavior of physical quantity is being studied in other frames of reference.

We have referred to coefficients of cyclical elasticity as measures of the relative responsiveness of physical volume to price changes and to other economic forces operating in the framework of business cycles. For most commodities the 'other forces' are usually more potent than the price changes. Where this is true quantity and price are in fact both dependent variables, changing under the impact of major cyclical forces. Under these circumstances the coefficient of cyclical elasticity may be thought of as a measure of the *differential responsiveness* of physical volume, the coefficient of cyclical flexibility as a measure of the *differential responsiveness* of unit prices. In each case the change in the other factor (e.g., the change in price, if elasticity of quantities is in question) is to be thought of as a standard of reference rather than as a primary causal influence. (On the supply side, of course, rising prices are a stimulus to increased output, falling prices a stimulus to output reduction. Here the prices are a link in a chain of factors influencing output.) The traditional coefficient of elasticity of demand is conceived of as

---

is playing a dependent role, price and other economic forces being the independent variables in the cyclical processes under discussion. There is, in fact, mutual interaction. However, since the 'dependent' variable is the physical quantity of a single commodity, while the price of that commodity and all other economic forces are cast in the role of independent variables, the usage here employed seems justifiable.

A stage coefficient, we should note, is computed from the reference cycle relatives for two successive stages (see Table 2). For interstage period I-II, for example, the coefficient of elasticity is the ratio of the relative rates of change—quantity to price—at the midpoint of the line joining the quantity and price observations for stages I and II. So derived, it is identical with a coefficient of arc elasticity.

10 An alternative 'full cycle' measure of the relative responsiveness of quantities and prices to the forces of business cycles could be obtained from the ratios of the cyclical amplitudes of these two factors.

a measure of the responsiveness of the quantity factor to a change in price, all other factors being assumed constant. In practice the complete constancy of other factors can never be realized. Indeed, when price and quantity movements are being studied in the framework of business cycles these other factors are generally dominant. Hence the concept of differential responsiveness is more appropriate than is that of direct functional dependence of quantity on price, or of price on quantity.

When elasticity is being measured in a temporal framework a symbol other than the conventional η should be employed. We use e ($e = y/x \cdot dx/dy$, where x represents quantity and y price). When e is greater than 1 quantity is *elastic* (i.e., more responsive than price to the impinging forces); when e is less than 1 quantity is *inelastic*. The use of this conventional distinction is justified when the context makes clear that the reference is to stage elasticity, phase elasticity, or to elasticity in some other temporal framework.

One further distinction is necessary. The general relations between price and quantity changes, over time, with which we deal may be *positive* (prices and quantities increase, concurrently, or decrease, concurrently) or *inverse* (prices and quantities move in opposite directions). When we seek to define quantity behavior, we may have behavior that is elastic and positive or inverse, or inelastic and positive or inverse. As the formula indicates, quantity behavior is always defined with reference to corresponding changes in unit prices.

In the definition of price behavior, in relation to corresponding quantity changes, we use the term *flexibility*, and the coefficient f ($f = x/y \cdot dy/dx$, where y represents price and x quantity). In doing so we are using the term first employed by Moore, but giving it the wider meaning that goes with the inclusion of changes over time. Here, as with elasticity, we qualify the term to indicate the temporal framework within which the responsiveness of prices is being studied, saying stage flexibility, phase flexibility, or full cycle flexibility. We shall regard prices as *flexible* when f is greater than 1, *inflexible* when f is less than 1, flexibility as *positive* when price and quantity movements are in the same direction, *inverse* when the movements are in opposite directions.

This extension of certain traditional concepts relating to co-ordinated price and quantity movements makes possible a wider application of these tools of analysis. It is necessary, however, to define precisely the conditions under which price-quantity relations are being studied in any specific case. The central feature of the procedure is that time is expressly introduced and that we are studying the behavior of quantity and unit prices in a complex of economic changes, including among others those represented by conventional demand and supply schedules. In particular, we emphasize the need of defining the temporal frame within which related price and quantity movements are being studied. Thus we might be concerned with concurrent seasonal movements of prices and quantities, with concurrent movements of prices and quantities during cycles in general business, with changes occurring in longer cycles, or with concurrent secular movements of prices and quantities. It is clear that the meaning to be attached to a statement such as 'The price of commodity A is inflexible, positively' or 'The output of commodity A is elastic, inversely' depends upon the framework within which the relative movements are being studied. The price of a commodity might be inflexible, in-versely, when studied in a seasonal framework; it might be flexible, positively, when studied in the reference cycle frame-work; it might be flexible, inversely, when movements over several decades were studied. In each case, it will be under-stood, the reference is to the behavior of prices relative to corresponding movements of quantities.

With these explanations in mind we turn to measures de-scribing the movements of merchant pig iron production and the behavior of pig iron prices in the framework of reference cycles. The coefficients in Table 4 are derived from the aver-age pattern of pig iron price and quantity movements during nine cycles in general business occurring between 1904 and 1938 (see Chart 2, Fig. 1).

The over-all measures indicate that merchant pig iron pro-duction is highly responsive to the forces of business cycles.

TABLE 4

Coefficients of Elasticity of Merchant Pig Iron Production and
Flexibility of Pig Iron Prices, Nine Business Cycles, 1904-1938

STAGE MEASURES
Interstage Period

	I-II	II-III	III-IV	IV-V	V-VI	VI-VII	VII-VIII	VIII-IX
Elasticity (e)	+4.71	+1.75	+1.13	+1.97	+0.22	+2.66	+2.99	+3.59
Flexibility (f)	+0.21	+0.57	+0.88	+0.51	+4.54	+0.38	+0.33	+0.28

PHASE MEASURES

	Expansion (I-V)	Contraction (V-IX)	FULL CYCLE MEASURE Av. of expansion and contraction
Elasticity (e)	+1.79	+2.55	+2.17
Flexibility (f)	+0.56	+0.39	+0.46

The coefficient of full cycle elasticity (+2.17) shows that both quantities and prices move, on the average, in the same direction during cycles in general business, rates of change in production being more than twice as great as concurrent rates of change in prices (i.e., for every change of 1 percent in pig iron prices there is on the average a change of 2.17 percent in merchant pig iron production, in the same direction). The corresponding coefficient of full cycle price flexibility is +0.46. The separate entries for expansion and contraction indicate that quantity is elastic, positively, and that prices are inflexible, positively, in both cyclical phases, but that the phase elasticity of quantities is greater and the phase flexibility of prices is less during contraction than during expansion.

The measures for the separate interstage periods reveal high elasticity of production (and relatively inflexible prices) in the first period of reference expansion (i.e., between stages I and II). Thereafter, during general business expansion, the degree of elasticity of production declines (the decline being checked, however, between stages IV and V) and the degree of flexibility of prices increases, but output shows relatively greater rates of change than price during all periods of expansion, up to the peak. Between stages V and VI merchant pig iron production declines only slightly and the coefficient e has a very low value (+0.22). During the remaining interstage periods of reference contraction pig iron production is highly, and in accelerating degree, elastic in response to cyclical forces, and the stage flexibility of prices steadily declines. The resistances to price rise (as here measured in relation to quantity changes) are strongest during the early stages of general business expansion; the resistances to pig iron price declines (relative to quantity reductions) increase in strength as contraction develops.

Outlays of Buyers and Revenues of Sellers in Business Cycles

We have referred in Chapter 1 to the procedure by which measures of the aggregate value of a given commodity can be estimated from data on the number of units of the commodity produced during a stated period and its average unit price.[11] Cyclical changes in such values are of clear significance in studying business cycles. They measure the volume of payments, the monetary counterpart of the stream of physical goods and services. These payments may be thought of as constituting the outlays of buyers, or the revenues of sellers. We may study the interaction of prices and quantities as components of changes in outlays and in revenues, therefore, and thus throw new light on the patterns of joint behavior described in preceding sections.

In tracing changes in the aggregate value of a commodity and in its two components, we use average rates of change per month, from stage to stage of reference cycles. These monthly rate-of-change figures for merchant pig iron, derived from the averages of reference cycle relatives in Table 2, are given in Table 5.

The record for pig iron values shows a series rising fairly rapidly during the initial period of expansion (at 2.7 per month, in terms of reference cycle relatives), with some retardation after stage II, and quite rapid increases between stages III and V. In the last period of expansion, before the peak of the reference cycle, the maximum rate of advance is reached. This is 4.5 per month—a figure that may be interpreted as 4.5 percent,

---

11 In this study values have been computed from monthly price and quantity records for individual commodities. The derived value series have then been analyzed in the reference cycle framework.

TABLE 5

Average Monthly Interstage Changes in Prices, Quantities, and Values of Merchant Pig Iron, Nine Business Cycles, 1904-1938

INTERSTAGE PERIOD	PRICE	QUANTITY	VALUE
I-II	+0.6	+2.8	+2.7
II-III	+1.1	+1.8	+2.4
III-IV	+1.8	+2.3	+4.2
IV-V	+1.3	+2.6	+4.5
V-VI	—1.0	—0.2	—1.5
VI-VII	—1.5	—4.1	—5.9
VII-VIII	—1.8	—5.0	—6.1
VIII-IX	—1.2	—3.0	—3.8

Since each of these changes is computed on the reference cycle average as base and not on the initial stage of each period as base, apparent numerical discrepancies among the rates for price, quantity, and value may occur.

if we remember that the base of the percentage for a given reference cycle is the average of all the monthly figures for pig iron values for that cycle. Recession sets in relatively slowly, values declining at a rate of 1.5 per month between stages V and VI. The next two periods of contraction bring sharp declines, reaching a rate of 6.1 between stages VII and VIII. There is a notable diminution of the rate of decline from stage VIII to the terminal trough at IX.

Examination of the figures for prices and quantities that parallel the value entries indicates the role of each component, in the expansion and contraction of pig iron values. Increases in quantities dominate heavily, in the first period of expansion in values, price advances playing a minor part. Between stages II and III there is appreciable retardation in the rate of increase in output; the price rise is accelerated. The quantity factor is dominant in pushing up monetary values throughout the phase of expansion, but prices become increasingly important as a boosting factor up to stage IV of reference expansion. In the final period of expansion the rate of price advance is checked; output continues to accelerate.

On recession prices exert the main pressure in the first slow decline in the monetary value of merchant pig iron produced. Production is only slightly reduced between stages V and VI. After contraction is well started (i.e., after stage VI of the reference cycle) the production series again takes charge, and forces monetary values down steadily, and at a high monthly rate, for the three succeeding periods of general business contraction. The maximum rates of production decline, it is to be noted, are substantially greater than the maximum rates of increase during the phase of expansion. Prices decline also, during reference contraction, but at a monthly rate that is fairly steady and close to the rates prevailing during the later stages of expansion. With recovery quantity changes provide the major stimulus to value advances, contributing rather more than unit price advances to swelling values in business expansion. But their strongest push on values is felt during the three final periods of contraction when they are almost three times as important as prices in causing aggregate values of merchant pig iron to tumble.

PRICE-QUANTITY PATTERNS IN BUSINESS CYCLES

T**HE** method of defining the movements of commodity prices and quantities in business cycles described in the preceding chapter has been applied to each of the 64 commodities included in this study.[1] In appraising the results we may examine measures for individual commodities or averages for the entire group and its subdivisions. This discussion is confined, in the main, to averages defining the characteristic behavior of broad categories of goods. The present chapter deals with the interplay of prices and quantities during cycles in general business. The next chapter deals with commodity values, that is, with the patterns of buyers' outlays and sellers' revenues during business cycles. Throughout we are viewing the movements of these economic variables in the framework of reference cycles—a frame provided by the expansions and contractions of business at large.[2]

---

[1] Basic cyclical measurements for individual commodities will be published in a later monograph. Brief descriptions of the price and quantity series employed are given in Appendix Table 1. The number of separate commodities included is actually 56; two different sets of quantity records are used for each of 8 commodities. The 64 combinations included are those for which generally comparable price and physical volume data are available, on a monthly basis. The periods covered range from 14 to 80 years. Although the sample is limited it is large enough to give some substantive content to the averages and aggregates derived from it. The total value of the commodities included constituted in 1937 about one-third of the aggregate value of all agricultural commodities, raw minerals, and manufactured goods produced in the United States. The sample is not presented, however, as one containing in due proportions representatives of the various kinds of goods produced and exchanged in the United States in a given year.

It will be clear to a reader examining the detailed descriptions of the price and quantity series employed that the records for different commodities are by no means fully comparable. Some of the quantity series relate to production, some to imports, some to receipts at central markets, some to consumption, some to shipments. The price series are alike in that all relate to wholesale markets, but these markets vary widely in character, and in their place in the productive-distributive process. These limitations of the basic data are to be borne in mind in interpreting the interactions of prices and quantities and the apparent movements of monetary outlays. The derived measures are to be looked upon as approximations, only, to those the economic analyst would like to have.

[2] In the interpretation of the findings discussed in this section the reader will bear in mind the character of this framework. In particular, he will note the

Individual Commodities

For light on the character of the patterns generated by correlated movements of commodity prices and quantities in business cycles and on the economic adjustments effected through these two factors, we turn first to a summary of results covering observations on 64 individual commodities. Table 6 shows the magnitude of the joint cyclical variability of prices and quantities for each of the commodities covered, and indicates the commodities for which the movements of prices or quantities, or of the two factors combined, appear to represent a trustworthy (i.e., a statistically significant) cyclical pattern.

The average patterns for the 64 commodities in Table 6 show an extraordinarily wide range in the amplitudes of the combined price-quantity movements during reference cycles. From 167, the joint variability of flour, the measures rise to 11,519 for coke. The range above the median (1,640) is very much wider than the range below. Products of heavy industry predominate among the 32 that lie above the median. These are, typically, the products for which quantities produced, or prices, or both, are peculiarly sensitive to business cycles. Yet in this upper group are also wool, potatoes, lard, cotton, and a few other commodities not originating in the heavy industry sector of the economy. Commodities of agricultural origin predominate in the lower half of the table, though here, in turn, are some industrial products, notably coal, tin, zinc sheet, and cement.

In these measures of joint variability we have the effects, intermixed, of true cyclical movements of prices or quantities, or of the two combined, and of fluctuations unrelated to business cycles. We have attempted to distinguish the cyclically

---

retention of intracycle trends. These trends are conceived to be elements of the data on which business judgments and operating decisions are based, and therefore properly to be retained in our study of the related patterns of price and quantity movements. For our sample of production and price series, and of business cycles, production trends were rising, on the average (at a rate of 0.1 percent of the average reference cycle base per month), and price trends were declining (at an average rate of 0.1 percent per month). These trend factors accentuate somewhat the lifting influence of production during business expansions and the depressing influence of prices during business contractions.

TABLE 6

64 Commodities in Order of Joint Cyclical Variability of Prices and Quantities in Reference Framework

	JOINT VARIABILITY		JOINT VARIABILITY
*Coke	11,519	*Pork	1,630
*Iron ore	8,107	*Tin	1,628
*Glass	7,260	*Silk, raw	1,565
*Steel, scrap	6,851	*Coal, bituminous	1,511
*Pig iron (merchant)	6,477	*Sheep (slaughter)	1,477
*Steel, plates	5,538	*Asphalt	1,439
*Steel, sheet	5,392	*Zinc, sheet	1,362
*Steel, structural	5,140	*Leather	1,212
*Steel, billets	4,790	*Butter (production)	1,045
*Lumber, fir	4,728	*Paper index	1,033
*Wool, raw	4,508	*Hogs (receipts)	987
*Copper	4,387	*Meat index	936
*Steel, rails	4,227	*Petroleum (Appalachian)	819
*Autos, passenger	4,090	*Sheep (receipts)	806
*Pig iron (total)	3,784	*Silk, yarn	761
*Milk, condensed	3,245	*Cotton (exports)	708
*Cottonseed oil, crude	2,985	*Butter (receipts)	665
*Worsted yarn	2,970	*Hogs (slaughter)	631
Potatoes	2,857	*Cattle (slaughter)	621
*Linseed oil	2,832	*Cattle (receipts)	583
*Cotton, yarn	2,811	Flour (production)	577
*Gasoline	2,759	*Cement	533
*Lubricants	2,726	*Beef	527
Cottonseed oil, refined	2,714	*Coffee	519
*Petroleum (total)	2,674	*Milk, evaporated	504
*Corn	2,665	*Coal, anthracite	473
Lard	2,634	*Milk, raw	364
*Rubber	2,581	Shoes	351
*Cotton (consumption)	2,274	Eggs	337
*Zinc, raw	2,194	Bread	207
Hides	1,666	Sugar	192
*Lead	1,649	Flour (shipments)	167

Certain commodities appear twice in this record. In each of these cases different physical volume series have been available, for combination with series measuring the prices of the commodity in question. Thus the production of merchant pig iron, for which records are available for nine business cycles between 1904 and 1938, has been paired with a composite pig iron price series to give one of our combinations; the total production of pig iron, for which data cover 16 business cycles between 1879 and 1938, has been paired with the price of pig iron in Eastern Pennsylvania to give another combination. Total petroleum production (covering 6 cycles) is a member of one combination, while Appalachian production (covering 13 cycles) enters into another. The parenthetical references in Table 6 and other tables define the physical volume series entering into these different combinations.

* Cyclical variability significant.

significant movements from others. Fifty-four of the commodities listed in Table 6 have patterns of behavior sufficiently consistent to justify the conclusion that they were generated by truly cyclical forces.[3] The commodities with relatively high joint variability predominate in the 'significant' list, but many articles on this list fall below the median, in amplitude of variability. Raw milk, with a joint variability of only 364, has a significant pattern; for potatoes, with a joint variability of 2,857, the average pattern is not significant. The explanation is that for milk the fluctuations, though small, are relatively consistent in 12 business cycles; for potatoes the record, which covers only 5 business cycles, is one of wide but erratic movements.

This survey of measures of amplitude has given some indication of the nature of the materials available to us in studying the correlated interactions of commodity prices and quantities in business cycles. In Table 7 we have a series of measures indicative of the part price has played in these interactions. Here, again, the range is very wide. For petroleum (this series is for the Appalachian field alone) and potatoes, at one end of the scale, cyclical fluctuations in the price factor accounted for 98 percent of the joint variability of prices and quantities, quantity fluctuations for 2 percent. (The reference, of course, is to variability that is related to cycles in general business. The method of averaging in the reference cycle framework tends to offset fluctuations not consistently associated with business cycles.) Passenger automobiles and iron ore were at the other extreme; price fluctuations contributed only 1 percent, while

[3] In the interpretation of these results it must be remembered that the measure of joint variability for each commodity is derived from the average price-quantity pattern (the counterpart of the pattern for merchant pig iron in Table 2). In a given case this average may represent a highly consistent pattern, repeated with only slight differences from cycle to cycle, or a pattern from which there is wide deviation from cycle to cycle. When this deviation is wide, the average pattern is not significant; when the deviation from cycle to cycle is moderate, and there is a fairly high degree of consistency in the patterns traced by price-quantity movements in successive cycles, significant average patterns emerge.

The criterion of significance is a composite one, involving tests of prices, quantities, and values of individual commodities. These tests are discussed in detail in a monograph scheduled for later publication.

quantity fluctuations accounted for 99 percent, of the combined variability. For 37 of the 64 commodities the price contribution was more than 50 percent of the total. Prices varied more than quantities, in their cyclical movements, for slightly more than half of the sample.

We discuss below distinctive group behavior. Here we note the dominance of agricultural products in that group of the entries in Table 7 for which the price contribution is more than 75 percent of the joint variability. Of the 15 commodities

TABLE 7

64 Commodities in Order of Price Contribution to
Joint Cyclical Variability in Reference Framework

	PRICE CONTRIBUTION (percent)		PRICE CONTRIBUTION (percent)
*Petroleum (Appalachian)	98	*Cotton (exports)	55
Potatoes	98	*Leather	55
*Meat index	95	*Milk, evaporated	54
*Hogs (slaughter)	92	*Copper	51
*Sheep (slaughter)	92	*Linseed oil	51
*Corn	91	*Gasoline	49
*Pork	89	*Zinc, raw	49
*Cottonseed oil, crude	88	*Milk, raw	48
Flour (production)	88	*Worsted yarn	48
Cottonseed oil, refined	86	*Coffee	46
Eggs	86	*Steel, scrap	44
*Beef	84	*Coal, anthracite	43
*Butter (production)	83	*Coal, bituminous	38
Lard	81	*Cement	37
*Lubricants	78	*Cattle (receipts)	31
*Cotton, yarn	75	*Coke	28
*Hogs (receipts)	75	*Pig iron (total)	21
*Butter (receipts)	74	*Steel, billets	20
*Silk, raw	73	*Pig iron (merchant)	19
Sugar	73	*Paper index	18
Hides	71	*Tin	18
*Cattle (slaughter)	69	*Zinc, sheet	18
*Cotton (consumption)	69	*Steel, structural	14
*Sheep (receipts)	67	*Steel, rails	8
*Petroleum (total)	66	*Glass	6
*Rubber	66	*Steel, sheet	6
*Silk, yarn	66	*Milk, condensed	5
Bread	65	*Asphalt	3
*Lumber, fir	59	Shoes	3
*Lead	58	*Steel, plates	2
Flour (shipments)	57	*Autos, passenger	1
*Wool, raw	57	*Iron ore	1

* Cyclical variability significant.

in this quarter 13 are of agricultural origin. The other 2, petroleum and lubricants, are minerals, but they resemble agricultural products in one important respect—producers cannot effect prompt changes in supply, on the basis of short-term market prospects. The entries in the bottom quarter, in contrast, are predominantly products of the heavy, metal-working industries. (Paper, condensed milk and shoes are outstanding exceptions.) Production of these articles is controlled on the basis of business prospects; the contribution of quantity fluctuations to joint variability is outstanding.

The aggregate record of related changes in commodity prices and quantities during business cycles is summarized in Table 8, Part 1. For 60 of the 64 commodities prices rose during the phase of general business expansion. (This statement applies, of course, to average patterns of behavior for individual commodities, not to behavior during any particular cycle.) For 47 of these there was a concurrent rise in quantities produced (or traded, or consumed). Quantities of 13 commodities showed no net change, or fell. In addition, quantities rose for 4 commodities for which prices did not rise. We have here a good summary picture of the response of commodity markets to the forces of business expansion. For roughly three-quarters of our list of commodities the push of revival is reflected in both unit prices and number of units produced. The remaining quarter is composed predominantly of goods for which prices rose while output did not. These observations indicate a more general positive response of prices than of quantities to expansion.[4] Yet of the 47 for which both factors advanced, 29 showed sharper rises in quantities than in prices. The net effect, indeed, of expansion, in terms of these average patterns of behavior, was to raise quantities more than prices from their relative standings at the preceding low point in general business. The participation of prices in expansions is more general but advances in quantities are more pronounced in a majority of the individual cases studied.[5]

[4] The response of physical quantities to business cycles takes the form of an inverted pattern for some commodities, e.g., butter receipts, cotton exports.
[5] Examination of records for larger samples of production and price series lends support to the second part of this statement although the lack of comparability

TABLE 8

Related Movements of Prices and Quantities in Reference Expansion and Contraction

PART 1

	No. OF COMMODITIES
A: REFERENCE EXPANSION (STAGES I-V)	
1) Classification by price movements	
Commodities for which prices show net rise	60
and quantities rise more than price	29
and quantities rise less than price	18
and quantities show no net change	2
and quantities fall	11
Commodities for which prices show no net change and quantities rise	2
Commodities for which prices show net fall and quantities rise	2
Total	64
2) Classification by quantity movements	
Commodities for which quantities show net rise	51
and prices rise more than quantity	18
and prices rise less than quantity	29
and prices show no net change	2
and prices fall	2
Commodities for which quantities show no net change and prices rise	2
Commodities for which quantities show net fall and prices rise	11
Total	64
B: REFERENCE CONTRACTION (STAGES V-IX)	
1) Classification by price movements	
Commodities for which prices show net fall	63
and quantities fall more than price	23
and quantities fall less than price	19
and quantities rise	21
Commodities for which prices show net rise and quantities fall	1
Total	64
2) Classification by quantity movements	
Commodities for which quantities show net fall	43
and prices fall more than quantity	19
and prices fall less than quantity	23
and prices rise	1
Commodities for which quantities show net rise and prices fall	21
Total	64

TABLE 8 (cont.)

PART 2

A: REFERENCE EXPANSION (STAGES I-V)

COMMODITIES FOR WHICH PRICES SHOW NET RISE

More than price (29)	Quantities Rise Less than price (18)	Quantities Show no Net Change (2)	Quantities Fall (11)
*Cattle (receipts)	*Beef	*Hogs (slaughter)	Bread
*Cement	*Butter (production)	Sugar	*Butter (receipts)
*Coal, anthracite	*Cattle (slaughter)		*Cotton (exports)
*Coal, bituminous	*Corn		*Cottonseed oil, c⟩
*Coffee	*Cotton (consumption)		Cottonseed oil, ⟩
*Coke	*Cotton, yarn		Flour (productio⟩
*Copper	Eggs		Lard
Flour (shipments)	Hides		*Lumber, fir
*Gasoline	*Hogs (receipts)		*Milk, condensed
*Leather	*Lead		*Pork
*Linseed oil	*Lubricants		*Sheep (slaughter⟩
*Milk, evaporated	*Meat index		
*Paper index	*Milk, raw		
*Pig iron (merchant)	*Petroleum (Appalachian)		
*Pig iron (total)	*Petroleum (total)		
*Rubber	Potatoes		
Shoes	*Sheep (receipts)		
*Silk, yarn	*Silk, raw		
*Steel, billets			
*Steel, plates			
*Steel, rails			
*Steel, scrap			
*Steel, sheet			
*Steel, structural			
*Tin			
*Wool, raw			
*Worsted yarn			
*Zinc, raw			
*Zinc, sheet			

COMMODITIES FOR WHICH PRICES SH⟨

No Net Change, Quantities Rise (2)	Net Fall, Quantities Rise (2)
*Autos, passenger	*Asphalt
*Iron ore	*Glass

*Cyclical variability significant.

This story may be read, by individual commodities, in Table 8, Part 2. The goods for which quantities fall, or advance less than prices, are primarily of agricultural origin. Lumber, lead,

---

of the production and price series lessens the immediate relevance of this general body of evidence. The median advance of 241 production series between reference cycle stages I and V was 20.3 (in reference cycle relatives); the median advance of 132 price series was 8.0 (war cycles were excluded in summarizing the price records). The price movements were much more compact and uniform than the production movements, a condition evidenced by an interquartile range of 5.8 for the price series, at stage V, and a corresponding interquartile range of 17.0 for the production series.

TABLE 8, PART 2 (concl.)

B: REFERENCE CONTRACTION (STAGES V-IX)

COMMODITIES FOR WHICH PRICES SHOW NET FALL			COMMODITIES FOR WHICH PRICES SHOW NET RISE
Quantities Fall		Quantities Rise	Quantities Fall
More than price (23)	Less than price (19)	(21)	(1)
*Autos, passenger	*Asphalt	Bread	*Coal, anthracite
*Cement	*Beef	*Butter (production)	
*Coal, bituminous	*Cattle (receipts)	*Butter (receipts)	
*Coke	*Cattle (slaughter)	*Coffee	
Flour (shipments)	*Copper	*Cotton (exports)	
*Glass	*Corn	*Cottonseed oil, crude	
*Iron ore	*Cotton (consumption)	Cottonseed oil, refined	
*Leather	*Cotton, yarn	Eggs	
*Linseed oil	Hides	Flour (production)	
*Milk, condensed	*Lead	*Gasoline	
*Paper index	*Lubricants	*Hogs (receipts)	
*Pig iron (merchant)	*Lumber, fir	*Hogs (slaughter)	
*Pig iron (total)	*Petroleum (Appalachian)	Lard	
Shoes	*Petroleum (total)	*Meat index	
*Steel, billets	*Rubber	*Milk, evaporated	
*Steel, plates	*Silk, raw	*Milk, raw	
*Steel, rails	*Silk, yarn	*Pork	
*Steel, scrap	*Wool, raw	Potatoes	
*Steel, sheet	*Zinc, raw	*Sheep (receipts)	
*Steel, structural		*Sheep (slaughter)	
*Tin		Sugar	
*Worsted yarn			
*Zinc, sheet			

*Cyclical variability significant.

petroleum (2 series), and lubricants are the only exceptions among 31 commodities. For the industrial sector of the economy, typically, both prices and quantities respond to the push of general business recovery, but the advances in quantities are far sharper. This significant fact is obscured, in the general record, by the presence of many agricultural and a few petroleum products for which output is not responsive to cyclical forces.

Prices participate even more widely during general business contractions. Of the 64 commodities 63 were characterized, on the average, by declining prices. For only 43 did quantities fall. For approximately one-third of the goods here studied, that is, business contractions at large brought no absolute declines in physical output (or exchange). This pronounced contracyclical tendency during business contractions, in a large minority of quantity series, has no counterpart in the price series. Prices do not buck the cyclical tide, on either expansion or contraction, to nearly the same extent as quantities. The degree of price change in particular industries may be slight, but the movement is usually with the tide.

Here, also, the record is illuminated by the details for individual commodities (Table 8, Part 2). The contrast between the industrial and agricultural sectors of the economy is again sharp. Of the 40 commodities for which contraction brings gains in quantities, or declines less marked than those of prices, 31 are of agricultural origin.[6] Industrial products predominate among the goods for which quantities decline more sharply than prices.

The relations of quantity and price movements in business cycles are defined by the coefficients e and f (measuring elasticity and flexibility). For the present purpose it is convenient to present the results for individual commodities in order of their 'full cycle' elasticities (Table 9). The full cycle measures are supplemented by elasticity coefficients for the phases of expansion and contraction.

In interpreting the measures in Table 9 chief interest attaches to the coefficients for the phases of expansion and contraction. These are unequivocal in their meaning. The averaging process involved in deriving the full cycle measures introduces an element of ambiguity when the signs of the measures for expansion and contraction differ.

Of the 64 commodities 49 are marked by positive relations between price and quantity changes during the expansion phases of business cycles, 15 by inverse movements. In the main, that is, the general forces of business expansion that may be thought of as impinging from without on the markets for individual commodities override the tendencies toward inverse relations between quantities and prices that are characteristic of demand schedules and reenforce the positive relations gen-

6 The reader should note that the present sample is rather heavily weighted with agricultural products. Their relative importance is greater in the sample than in the economy at large.

TABLE 9

64 Commodities in Order of Elasticity of Quantities and, Inversely, in Order of Flexibility of Prices in Business Cycles

A: COMMODITIES FOR WHICH FULL CYCLE ELASTICITY IS POSITIVE

| | PHASE MEASURES, ELASTICITY | | FULL CYCLE MEASURES | |
	Expansion	Contraction	Elasticity	Flexibility
*Iron ore	+344.44	+28.60	+186.52[a]	+0.01
Shoes	+6.09	+7.62	+6.86	+0.15
*Steel, plates	+5.46	+7.74	+6.60	+0.15
Flour (shipments)	+5.80	+6.80	+6.30	+0.16
*Steel, sheet	+5.39	+3.81	+4.60	+0.22
*Steel, rails	+3.78	+2.49	+3.14	+0.32
*Paper index	+4.50	+1.75	+3.12	+0.32
*Steel, structural	+2.41	+3.42	+2.92	+0.34
*Cement	+1.39	+3.39	+2.39	+0.42
*Gasoline	+4.90	—0.25	+2.32	+0.43
*Steel, billets	+2.09	+2.27	+2.18	+0.46
*Pig iron (merchant)	+1.79	+2.55	+2.17	+0.46
*Rubber	+4.11	+0.15	+2.13	+0.47
*Zinc, sheet	+1.92	+2.24	+2.08	+0.48
*Coal, bituminous	+1.43	+2.64	+2.04	+0.49
*Pig iron (total)	+2.20	+1.87	+2.04	+0.49
*Milk, condensed	—0.44	+4.24	+1.90	+0.53
*Tin	+2.23	+1.57	+1.90	+0.53
*Glass	—7.00	+10.49	+1.74	+0.57
*Coke	+1.34	+1.92	+1.63	+0.61
*Linseed oil	+1.92	+1.20	+1.56	+0.64
*Leather	+1.75	+1.07	+1.41	+0.71
*Worsted yarn	+1.43	+1.05	+1.24	+0.81
*Steel, scrap	+1.27	+1.08	+1.18	+0.85
*Wool, raw	+1.44	+0.87	+1.16	+0.86
*Cattle (receipts)	+1.57	+0.58	+1.08	+0.93
*Silk, yarn	+1.58	+0.56	+1.07	+0.93
*Copper	+1.22	+0.83	+1.02	+0.98
*Zinc, raw	+1.02	+0.87	+0.94	+1.06
*Lead	+0.91	+0.80	+0.86	+1.16
*Cotton (consumption)	+0.88	+0.80	+0.84	+1.19
*Cattle (slaughter)	+0.77	+0.81	+0.79	+1.27
*Beef	+0.85	+0.40	+0.62	+1.61
*Cotton, yarn	+0.62	+0.62	+0.62	+1.61
Hides	+0.59	+0.58	+0.58	+1.72
*Lubricants	+0.78	+0.31	+0.54	+1.85
*Milk, evaporated	+1.19	—0.28	+0.46	+2.17
*Coffee	+2.11	—1.25	+0.43	+2.33
*Silk, raw	+0.72	+0.09	+0.40	+2.50
*Petroleum (total)	+0.63	+0.08	+0.36	+2.78
*Lumber, fir	—0.05	+0.65	+0.30	+3.33
*Corn	+0.17	+0.04	+0.10	+10.00
*Petroleum (Appalachian)	+0.04	+0.16	+0.10	+10.00
*Meat index	+0.13	—0.08	+0.02	+50.00

PRICE-QUANTITY INTERACTIONS

TABLE 9 (concl.)

B: COMMODITIES FOR WHICH FULL CYCLE ELASTICITY IS NEGATIVE

| | PHASE MEASURES, ELASTICITY | | FULL CYCLE MEASURES | |
	Expansion	Contraction	Elasticity	Flexibility
Potatoes	+0.10	—0.13	—0.02	—50.00
*Sheep (receipts)	+0.27	—0.45	—0.09	—11.11
*Milk, raw	+0.62	—0.81	—0.10	—10.00
*Hogs (slaughter)	+0.01	—0.23	—0.11	—9.09
*Butter (production)	+0.16	—0.39	—0.12	—8.33
Eggs	+0.08	—0.33	—0.12	—8.33
*Hogs (receipts)	+0.28	—0.57	—0.14	—7.14
Flour (production)	—0.14	—0.17	—0.16	—6.25
*Cottonseed oil, crude	—0.21	—0.21	—0.21	—4.76
Cottonseed oil, refined	—0.15	—0.28	—0.22	—4.55
*Pork	—0.18	—0.28	—0.23	—4.35
*Sheep (slaughter)	—0.13	—0.33	—0.23	—4.35
*Coal, anthracite	+2.15	—2.65	—0.25	—4.00
Sugar	—0.01	—0.84	—0.42	—2.38
Lard	—1.27	—0.24	—0.76	—1.32
*Butter (receipts)	—0.76	—0.81	—0.78	—1.28
*Cotton (exports)	—0.89	—0.90	—0.90	—1.11
Bread	—0.21	—2.94	—1.58	—0.63
*Asphalt	—34.75	+0.44	—17.16	—0.06
*Autos, passenger	—132.27	+22.00	—55.14[a]	—0.02

For convenience of classification these coefficients are given to two decimal places. This does not imply accuracy to the second decimal place.

* Cyclical variability significant.

a When the measure of price change during expansion or contraction is close to zero the coefficient of elasticity may be very large. It will, moreover, be subject to considerable variation in magnitude, and to alteration in sign, with slight shifts in the price measure. In such cases the sign of the coefficient may not be particularly revealing, without reference to the underlying measurements. Thus iron ore and automobiles, which stand at opposite ends of Table 9, were much alike in their cyclical movements, with wide, positively conforming quantity changes and slight price changes. In phases of expansion, however, the net movement of iron ore prices, as averaged for all cycles, was positive (+0.2 in reference cycle relatives) while the net movement of automobile prices was negative (—0.5). This minor difference in net price changes leads to the difference in the signs of the two coefficients of elasticity. Of the commodities listed only flour, in addition to automobiles and iron ore, was marked by a net price change, in expansion or contraction, of less than 1.

Coefficients of price flexibility would be similarly affected by slight shifts in the net movements of the quantity factor, when the quantity measure is close to zero. Eggs, hogs (slaughter), and sugar were characterized by net changes in physical volume of less than 1, in periods of expansion or contraction.

Under the same conditions (i.e., when either the price or quantity measure is about zero) full cycle measures of elasticity and flexibility are subject to similar variations with slight shifts in the basic measures. To this variability is added a technical difficulty in obtaining an unequivocal average when the phase coefficients differ in sign. Full cycle coefficients of elasticity and flexibility derived by averaging phase coefficients of opposite sign are not open to interpretation in customary terms.

erally prevailing on the supply side. Among the commodities having positive price and quantity relations the range of the coefficients of elasticity is from +344.44 for iron ore to +0.01 for hogs. The negative coefficients range from −132.27 for passenger automobiles to −0.01 for sugar. Durables, chiefly metal products, predominate among the goods that are elastic in their quantity movements, but shoes, flour, paper, and gasoline are high on this list. Quantity inelasticity and high price flexibility (positive or inverse) are found among farm products and foods, though raw silk, petroleum, lumber, and lead appear also in this part of the list.

The elasticity measurements for the phase of contraction range, on the positive side, from +28.60 for iron ore to +0.04 for corn, on the negative side, from −2.94 for bread to −0.08 for meat. Forty-two of the 64 commodities show positive relations between price and quantity changes, 22 negative relations. In contraction, as in expansion, forces related to business cycles are generally stronger than the more specific forces making for inverse relations between prices and quantities. We note, too, that the commodities marked by high elasticity of quantities in expansion usually show above-average elasticity in contraction, while inelasticity in expansion is paired with inelasticity in contraction. Asphalt, gasoline, and rubber, all of which are highly elastic in expansion and inelastic in contraction, are notable exceptions. The proportion of commodities for which quantities are elastic (and price inflexible) is somewhat higher in expansion than in contraction (34 out of 64 in expansion, 26 out of 64 in contraction). For the sample of commodities here studied, a majority is marked by volume elasticity in expansion, by price flexibility in contraction. Quantities are freer to rise than are prices; prices are freer to fall than are quantities. Finally, we observe that in contraction, as in expansion, an extraordinary range of variation among these coefficients reflects wide diversity in the relative responsiveness of commodity prices and quantities to the forces of business cycles and to pressures originating in particular markets.

Composite Records

From these individual records we pass to the general picture of the related movements of commodity prices and quantities during business cycles. A graphic presentation of the composite pattern is given in Chart 3,[7] based upon the average standing of the 64 commodities here studied at each of nine stages of business cycles. The coordinates and derived descriptive measurements appear in Table 10.[8] These measures and those in

TABLE 10

Movements of Prices and Quantities in Business Cycles
All Commodities

A: AVERAGE STANDING AT REFERENCE CYCLE STAGES

	I	II	III	IV	V	VI	VII	VIII	IX
Price	94	99	104	110	112	110	99	91	90
Quantity	90	98	101	108	112	107	99	94	94

B: JOINT VARIABILITY IN REFERENCE CYCLES

		PERCENTAGE CONTRIBUTION TO JOINT VARIABILITY							
	JOINT	Full Cycle		Expansion			Contraction		
	VARIABILITY	p	q	p	q	p+q	p	q	p+q
Av. reference cycle pattern	1,005	57	43	20	24	44	37	19	56

the tables that follow, it must be emphasized, relate to the average behavior of many commodities in many business cycles. Just as there are differences from commodity to commodity, so are there differences from cycle to cycle. In the process of aggregating and averaging we deliberately subordinate these differences and search for general and persisting patterns of behavior. But such an over-all average, it is clear, cannot accord perfectly with the pattern for any particular commodity or with aggregate movements in any particular business cycle.

[7] Two methods of portraying such movements were noted in the preceding chapter. One involves the superimposing of price and quantity graphs, with an x-scale on which cyclical stages are marked off. We employ here a coordinate system, with reference cycle relatives for prices plotted on the y-scale, those for quantities plotted on the x-scale. While studying Chart 3, the reader may wish to examine the superimposed price and quantity graphs shown in Chart 5.

[8] In computing the coordinates that define the average pattern of price-quantity behavior, measures for individual commodities were equally weighted. No account was taken of differences in the number of cycles covered by the records for the various commodities.

Chart 3 reveals a pattern of price-quantity behavior generally characteristic of conforming series. Unit prices and quantities both increase between stages I and V of reference cycles, fall between stages V and IX. Neither movement is broken by shifts that reverse the general tide of expansion and contraction, but

CHART 3

Pattern of Related Price–Quantity Movements in Business Cycles, All Commodities

Averages by Cycle Stages

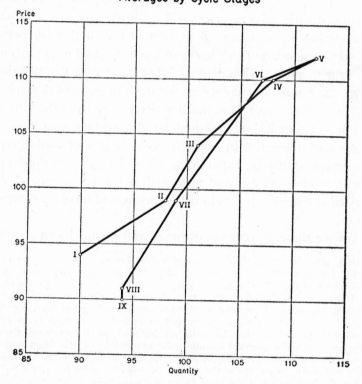

the decline in quantities is ended at stage VIII. Prices continue to decline at a low rate to stage IX.

The range of movement along the two scales of Chart 3 is the same, but the contributions of the price and quantity components to their combined variability is not the same. The averages defining the standing of the physical volume series at successive cyclical stages are more closely concentrated about their mean than are the price averages. Of the combined variability of prices and quantities 57 percent is attributable to price fluctuations, 43 percent to quantity movements.[9] Prices fluctuate more widely than quantities, in the sense that their wider deviations from the cyclical averages persist over more stages of the cycle than do the more extreme deviations of quantities.[10] This is true, indeed, of the contraction phase alone, but the full cycle measures reflect this condition.

The contributions of the two phases of business cycles to the combined variability of prices and quantities are also unequal. Contraction accounts for 56 percent of the total, with prices heavily preponderant, while expansion accounts for 44 percent, with the quantity component slightly greater than that of price. Since the point of reference in the measurement of deviations is the cycle average, this means that divergence from the kind of business 'normalcy' represented by the average standings of prices and quantities in business cycles is greater during contractions than during expansions. The chief factor in the divergence, as here defined and measured, is the persistence of depressed commodity prices in the later stages of business contraction.

We see these movements of prices and quantities in a some-

[9] Prices are subject to relatively greater fluctuations during war cycles than during peacetime cycles. The exclusion of records for war cycles for all commodities yields the following figures, which are to be compared with those given in Table 10, Part B. When war cycles are omitted, the joint variability of prices and quantities is reduced by about one-eighth. The percentage contributions of prices and quantities are changed to 44 and 56, respectively, as compared with 57 and 43 when all cycles are included. In the peacetime record, therefore, changes in physical quantities are responsible for the larger proportion of the combined variability of prices and quantities. The exclusion of war cycles serves also to accentuate the role of the quantity factor in expansions, to reduce the importance of the price factor in contractions.

		PERCENTAGE CONTRIBUTION TO JOINT VARIABILITY							
	JOINT	Full Cycle		Expansion			Contraction		
	VARIABILITY	p	q	p	q	p+q	p	q	p+q
Av. reference cycle pattern	878	44	56	17	31	48	27	25	52

[10] The use of squared deviations in deriving the aggregate measure of 'joint variability' gives extra weight to the sustained divergence of average prices from the reference cycle average.

what different light when we define the rates of change of the
two factors by interstage periods (Table 11). A sharp initial
rise occurs in quantities—indeed, the rate for this factor is at
its maximum for the cycle between stages I and II. Thereafter,
during expansion, the rate of increase in quantities is lower.
It drops substantially between stages II and III, then recovers
somewhat to stage V. During three of the four interstage periods
of expansion quantities increase more rapidly than prices, the
only exception being interstage period II-III. The initial drop
in quantities, after stage V, is sharp, again well above the rate
of decline in prices. Between stages VI and VII, however, the
price decline is accelerated. In three of the four interstage periods of contraction the rate of price decline exceeds the rate of
quantity decline. Maximum rates of price change for the whole

TABLE 11

Average Monthly Interstage Changes in Prices and
Quantities in Business Cycles, All Commodities

INTERSTAGE PERIOD	PRICE	QUANTITY
I-II	+1.1	+1.7
II-III	+0.6	+0.4
III-IV	+0.7	+0.9
IV-V	+0.6	+0.9
V-VI	—0.7	—1.6
VI-VII	—1.6	—1.1
VII-VIII	—1.3	—0.9
VIII-IX	—0.3	+0.1

The rates are derived from the average standings of prices and quantities of
64 commodities at reference stages (Table 10). The differences between the
standings (computed to one decimal place) at successive stages are divided by
the average number of months in the period in question, over the time span
of the present observations. Thus the average duration of interstage period I-II
is 4.6 months. (This is derived by dividing 2,394.5 months, the actual aggregate
of the months covered by records for the 64 commodities for the period between
stages I and II, by 520, the number of items in this aggregate.) Dividing the
difference between 94.3 and 99.2 the average standings of prices at stages I and
II by 4.6, we have +1.1 the average change in unit price, per month, for the 64
commodities. Measures are in terms of reference cycle relatives. The other entries in Table 11 were similarly derived. See Arthur F. Burns and Wesley C.
Mitchell, *Measuring Business Cycles*, Ch. 5, for a fuller explanation of the measure of interstage change.

The use of stage averages carried to one decimal place in deriving the entries
in Tables 11 and 12 accounts for certain minor differences between these tables
and Table 10. (The slight rise in quantity between stages VIII and IX is not
apparent in the rounded figures of Table 10.)

cycle, indeed, occur between stages VI and VIII. In the terminal period of contraction both prices and quantities are nearly immobile—a situation unlike that prevailing in the final stage of expansion, when both factors push upward. The reversal of direction at stage V is sharper and more pronounced for the quantity factor than is the turn of the tide when contraction gives way to expansion. Expansion gets under way with relatively sharp acceleration, it is true, but this follows a stage of semi-stagnation.[11]

From the average pattern of reference cycle behavior for all 64 commodities (Chart 5 and Table 10), we have derived measures of the elasticity of physical quantities and the flexibility of unit prices for interstage periods, for expansion and contraction, and for the full cycle (Table 12). The record for the full cycle shows that quantities and unit prices move in general in the same direction, under the pressure of cyclical forces, and differ but slightly in their average rates of change. By convention, we should classify the quantity movements as elastic (positively), the price movements as inflexible (positively), since the coefficient e is greater than unity while f is less than unity. But the difference is too small to be significant.

If we go behind the approximate equality of the price and quantity measures for the full cycle we find notable differences in behavior from phase to phase and from stage to stage of reference cycles. The phase coefficients tell an illuminating story of related quantity and price changes in business cycles. During

[11] The comments of this and the following paragraphs apply to the sample of 64 commodities for which price and quantity series are here compared. More comprehensive (but less comparable) price and physical volume index numbers show some differences of behavior. In particular, general index numbers of industrial production show acceleration of decline from interstage period V-VI to VI-VII. This is notably true of durable manufactured goods and of mining production. The general index of consumer goods production shows a maximum rate of decline in period V-VI, however. The acceleration of price decline shown by the present evidence is apparent also in the behavior of general price index numbers. (Cf. the rates of price change given in Ch. 5, note 9.)

The index of industrial production of the Federal Reserve Board, covering only five recent cycles, reveals no difference in the sharpness of reversal of movement at the peaks and troughs of business cycles; the more comprehensive Babson index of volume of business activity, covering eight business cycles, indicates semi-stagnation between stages VIII and IX and a much sharper reversal at peaks than at troughs.

TABLE 12

Measures of Elasticity of Quantities and
Flexibility of Prices in Business Cycles, All Commodities

STAGE MEASURES
Interstage Period

	I-II	II-III	III-IV	IV-V	V-VI	VI-VII	VII-VIII	VIII-IX
Elasticity	+1.59	+0.69	+1.34	+1.47	+2.34	+0.71	+0.69	—0.32
Flexibility	+0.63	+1.45	+0.75	+0.68	+0.43	+1.41	+1.45	—3.12

	PHASE MEASURES		FULL CYCLE MEASURE
	Expansion	Contraction	Av. of expansion and contraction
Elasticity	+1.25	+0.81	+1.01 a
Flexibility	+0.80	+1.23	+0.99 a

a For formal consistency between measures of elasticity and flexibility for the full cycle, as derived by averaging elasticity measures and their reciprocals for the separate phases of expansion and contraction, the geometric mean of arithmetic and harmonic means of the separate measures should be employed. The full cycle measures for all commodities are of this type. Full cycle measures for individual commodities and commodity groups given in other tables are derived by averaging (arithmetically) coefficients of elasticity for expansion and contraction. Flexibility coefficients for the full cycle are reciprocals of the coefficients of elasticity.

periods of general business expansion physical volume increases 1.25 percent for every 1 percent rise in price. During contractions commodity prices decline 1.23 percent, on the average, for every 1 percent fall in physical volume. We shall find wide differences among commodity groups in the correlated behavior of quantity and price, but for the aggregate of commodities here studied quantity is elastic, positively, in response to the stimulations of expansion and unit prices are flexible, positively, under the pressures of contraction.[12]

We trace these relations more closely in the measures for interstage periods. Quantities are elastic, relatively, in three of the four interstage periods of expansion (in period II-III alone

[12] The exclusion of war cycles, which are marked by relatively wide price movements, yields the following measures for all commodities. The elasticity of quantities is increased, the flexibility of prices substantially decreased, when war cycles are left out. Prices are more flexible in expansion than in contraction, but the coefficient f remains below unity, even in contraction, under peacetime conditions.

	PHASE MEASURES		FULL CYCLE
	Expansion	Contraction	MEASURE
Elasticity of quantities	+1.54	+1.02	+1.25
Flexibility of prices	+0.65	+0.98	+0.80

are prices more responsive than quantities to cyclical pressures), inelastic in three of the four interstage periods of contraction (in period V-VI alone are quantities more responsive than prices to cyclical pressures). All the interstage measures are positive (indicating direct relations between price and quantity changes) except that for the terminal period of contraction (VIII-IX). At this final stage prices are declining and quantities increasing, but the increase in quantity is relatively less rapid than the decline in price, and the coefficient *e* is below unity.

The coefficients for the eight interstage periods show a distinct and suggestive pattern of change. After the decline in the elasticity of quantities after stage II, there is a progressive increase in the stage elasticity of physical quantities (and a corresponding progressive decline in the flexibility of unit prices) between periods II-III and V-VI of reference cycles. We may think of these two factors as representing alternative means by which markets respond to and adapt themselves to the pressures of rising demand during business expansion, of declining demand during contraction. After the reversal of the second period, accommodations are effected in increasing degree through physical output. Prices become decreasingly flexible, relative to quantities. There is a sharp contrast indeed between the situation prevailing between stages II and III, when prices advance 1.45 percent for every 1 percent rise in quantity, and that in the final period of reference expansion (IV-V) when prices advance only 0.68 percent for every 1 percent rise in quantity. These growing strictures on prices, relative to the forces affecting output and sales, are a notable feature of the present evidence bearing on the later stages of business expansion.

In the first period of contraction (V-VI) quantities drop sharply, while prices decline but slightly. Thereafter the record is the exact opposite of that for expansion. There is a pronounced and progressive decline in the elasticity of quantities (and a progressive increase in the flexibility of unit prices). Quantity falls at a declining rate, relative to prices; prices decline at accelerating rates, relative to quantities. Between stages V and VI prices decline 0.43 percent for every 1 percent fall in quantities; between stages VII and VIII average unit prices fall 1.45 percent for every 1 percent fall in quantities. As general contraction spreads, and pervades the economy, resistances to continuing reductions in physical quantity are stronger, relatively, than the resistances to continuing price declines. Price is distinctly the more responsive factor, in all except the first period of business contraction.

Commodity Groups

In getting the average pattern of price-quantity behavior during business cycles we have thrown records for a wide variety of commodities into a single composite. The picture that emerges reflects the tides of cyclical change with rather high consistency. Certain suggestive differences between prices and quantities in their cyclical behavior have been discussed in preceding pages. We shall get more insight into these differences if we examine the market behavior of the various kinds of goods that make up our composite. Price-quantity patterns for sixteen major classes of goods are shown graphically in Chart 4.[13] (Each group pattern is derived by averaging the stage measurements defining the patterns of the individual commodities belonging to that group. Examples of individual commodity

[13] These groups are described in Appendix Table 2. The reader should note that certain of the groups are mutually exclusive (raw materials and manufactured goods; American farm products and products other than American farm products; crop and animal products, metals, and nonmetallic minerals; durable goods and nondurable goods). Other categories are not mutually exclusive. (Gasoline is both a producer good and a consumer good; so are coke, passenger automobiles, lubricants, and many other goods. Pig iron, passenger automobiles, lumber and other goods are both human consumption goods and goods intended for use in capital equipment or as building materials.) The commodity classes thus include overlapping and exclusive categories. Moreover, the categories cut across one another in diverse ways. Butter is a manufactured good, an American farm product, an animal product, a consumer good, a human consumption good, a nondurable good, and a food product.

The captions of the groups are largely self-explanatory. A consumer good is one that is in shape for final consumption; a producer good is one that is intended for instrumental use (in capital equipment) or one that requires further fabrication if it is intended for human consumption. A human consumption good is one that is intended for ultimate human consumption, either in its present shape or after further fabrication. Producer goods destined for human consumption are those that will become consumer goods after further fabrication. All categories except raw and manufactured goods cut across the raw-processed division. Thus American farm products include manufactured as well as primary products.

CHART 4

Patterns of Related Price-Quantity Movements in Business Cycles
Sixteen Major Commodity Groups — Averages by Cycle Stages

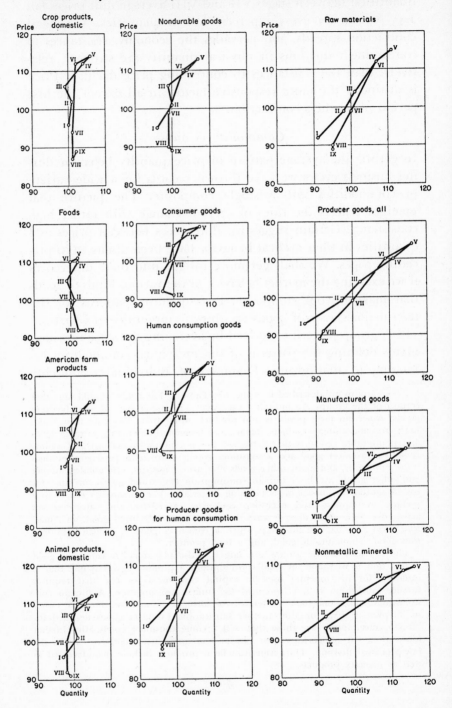

CHART 4 (continued)

Patterns of Related Price-Quantity Movements in Business Cycles
Sixteen Major Commodity Groups — Averages by Cycle Stages

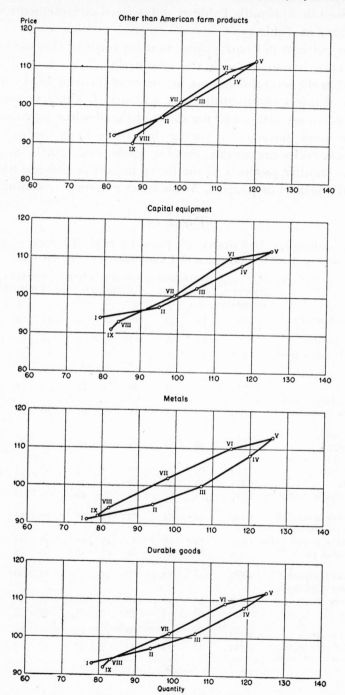

patterns are shown in Chart 2.) The coordinates here plotted are given in Appendix Table 3, and derived measurements are presented in Table 13.

The patterns in Chart 4 differ in many respects. One obvious difference has to do with the amplitude of the fluctuations traced in the several diagrams. Measures of the combined variability of prices and quantities are set forth in Table 14 where the groups are arrayed in the order of the absolute magnitude of the joint movements. Among the groups most sensitive to business cycles are metals, durable goods, and capital equipment—familiar products of the heavy industries that are traditionally princes or paupers. At the other extreme are consumer

TABLE 13

Measures Descriptive of Joint Cyclical Behavior
of Prices and Quantities, All Commodities and Groups

| | | PERCENTAGE CONTRIBUTION TO JOINT VARIABILITY | | | | | | | |
| | JOINT | Full cycle | | Expansion | | | Contraction | | |
	VARIABILITY	p	q	p	q	p+q	p	q	p+q
All commodities	1,005	57	43	20	24	44	37	19	56
Raw materials	1,155	69	31	27	17	44	42	14	56
Manufactured goods	940	41	59	12	33	45	29	26	55
American farm products	665	93	7	29	4	33	64	3	67
Other than American farm products	1,949	27	73	11	39	50	16	34	50
Crop products, domestic	887	96	4	29	3	32	67	1	68
Animal products, domestic	570	90	10	31	6	37	59	4	63
Metals	3,273	17	83	8	43	51	9	40	49
Nonmetallic minerals	1,345	32	68	13	36	49	19	32	51
Producer goods, all	1,440	46	54	17	29	46	29	25	54
Producer goods for human consumption	1,130	74	26	25	15	40	49	11	60
Consumer goods	445	80	20	21	11	32	59	9	68
Capital equipment	2,664	18	82	7	41	48	11	41	52
Human consumption goods	805	78	22	26	11	37	52	11	63
Foods	470	96	4	30	1	31	66	3	69
Durable goods	2,833	16	84	7	43	50	9	41	50
Nondurable goods	724	88	12	30	8	38	58	4	62

goods, foods, farm products, and nondurable goods. (Each group overlaps various other groups, of course.) The range of difference is wide; the joint variability of metals is more than seven times that of consumer goods.[14]

The entries in Table 14 indicate the magnitude of the cyclical fluctuations to which markets for various types of goods are exposed during cycles in general business. These fluctua-

TABLE 14

Commodity Groups in Order of Joint Cyclical
Variability of Prices and Quantities

	JOINT VARIABILITY
Metals	3,273
Durable goods	2,833
Capital equipment	2,664
Other than American farm products	1,949
Producer goods, all	1,440
Nonmetallic minerals	1,345
Raw materials	1,155
Producer goods for human consumption	1,130
All commodities	*1,005*
Manufactured goods	940
Crop products, domestic	887
Human consumption goods	805
Nondurable goods	724
American farm products	665
Animal products, domestic	570
Foods	470
Consumer goods	445

tions are composites of changing physical quantities and varying unit prices. Changes in either factor bring stimulation in their advances and uncertainty, approaching demoralization, in their rapid declines. The relative intensity of the combined effects of these two factors and the degree of alternating stimulation and depression to which producers of various classes of goods are exposed are suggested by the measures of joint varia-

[14] It will be recalled that the measure of joint variability is the sum of the squared deviations of individual observations from the point of averages. The process of squaring accentuates the differences. If we use, as an alternative measure of variation, the amplitude of the cyclical swings in monetary values, the range of difference is narrower, extending from a low of 34 for foods to a high of 138 for metals (these are reference cycle amplitudes). The two measures differ, of course, in derivation and meaning.

bility. But each of these is the sum of price and quantity components, and the groups differ widely in the relative importance of the two components. The graphs in Chart 4 and the entries in Table 15 illuminate the roles played by prices and quantities in these combined movements.

TABLE 15

Commodity Groups in Order of Price Contribution
to Joint Cyclical Variability of Prices and Quantities

	PRICE CONTRIBUTION (percent)
Crop products, domestic	96
Foods	96
American farm products	93
Animal products, domestic	90
Nondurable goods	88
Consumer goods	80
Human consumption goods	78
Producer goods for human consumption	74
Raw materials	69
All commodities	57
Producer goods, all	46
Manufactured goods	41
Nonmetallic minerals	32
Other than American farm products	27
Capital equipment	18
Metals	17
Durable goods	16

The patterns in Chart 4 are arranged in the order of the relative contributions of prices to the combined price-quantity variability. Movements on the vertical axis, it will be recalled, define price changes from stage to stage of reference cycles; movements on the horizontal axis define quantity changes. Thus the inclination of each group pattern serves as an index of the roles played by the two factors in the market adjustments during business cycles. At the top are products of domestic crops.[15] Price movements account for 96 percent of the combined cyclical variability of prices and quantities of crop products. Between stages III and VI alone do quantities appear to vary in any consistent way with the cyclical movements of general business.

15 Our quantity series define consumption, meltings, grindings, exports, shipments, and the production of various derived products measurable on a monthly basis, not the annual output of cotton, corn, and other crops.

For foods, animal products, farm products in general, and nondurable goods price movements are also predominantly responsible for the observed joint variability. All these categories overlap, of course, with agricultural products bulking large in each. It is characteristic of these goods that basic output is not readily controllable by producers during the periods covered by business cycles or that cost conditions are such that curtailment of output on short order is not expedient. Producers' commitments in respect of output are made well before the time of final production, and natural forces rather than human decisions are the chief factors operating thereafter. These conditions are clearly reflected in the price-quantity patterns for these types of goods, which are ranged almost vertically. Prices reflect the pressures of cyclical advances and absorb the shocks of cyclical declines. Quantities vary only slightly from stage to stage of business cycles. (There are, of course, fluctuations of considerable amplitude in most series measuring the output of agricultural products, but they do not agree regularly in timing with cycles in business at large. Hence the reference cycle patterns, which we are studying here, show but a small part of the amplitudes of the cycles specific to the various individual series.)

Goods intended for human consumption, such goods in final form for consumption, and the broad class of raw materials are also in the upper section of the chart (and of Table 15) with prices playing the chief role in cyclical adjustments. In markets close to the initial stage of extraction and to the final stage of consumption prices vary more than quantities during business cycles. The operative conditions are far from the same in these two types of market. The previously noted characteristics of supply place their impress on the primary markets; relative stability of consumption, particularly of nondurable goods, is a major circumstance influencing markets for consumption goods. But the net result is somewhat the same—relative constancy of quantities as business cycles run their course, relatively high variability of prices as demand waxes and wanes during the expansions and contractions of general business.

Markets intervening between initial production and final

consumption are heavily represented among the classes of goods listed in the lower half of Table 15 and depicted in the third and fourth columns of Chart 4. For producer goods (goods not yet in shape for final use in consumption and goods intended for instrumental use rather than direct consumption) price movements contribute only 46 percent to the joint variability of prices and quantities; quantity fluctuations contribute 54 percent. The price percentage is lower (41) for manufactured goods. It is much lower for metals and other minerals, for non-farm products, and for capital equipment. It is lowest of all for the general class of durable goods, 16 percent; the quantity contribution is 84 percent of the combined variability. The figure for durable goods in Chart 4 is closest to the horizontal, in its inclination. The quantity factor responds sensitively and immediately to the forces of general expansion and contraction; prices move uniformly and symmetrically, but the price movements are relatively modest.

For one important purpose we must go behind measures of relative price and quantity contributions, and study the absolute magnitudes of the two components (Table 16). The order of listing is slightly different from that in Table 15, but chief interest attaches to the widely different ranges of the two sets of absolute figures. For prices, the range extends from 37 percent below the all commodity average (consumer goods) to 49 percent above (crop products). On the quantity scale the measures of cyclical variability range from 96 percent below the all commodity average (foods) to 528 percent above (metals). The measures of average variability for prices and quantities are not far apart—the price average is slightly greater—but in their internal dispersion the two are poles apart. The meaning, of course, is that unit prices of commodities are far more homogeneous in the magnitude of their response to cyclical forces than are physical quantities. There are ties among prices that have no counterpart among physical series.

For all commodities the absolute variability of quantities is greater in the expansion phase of business cycles than in contraction (see Table 13 and Chart 3). A secular growth factor, together with a typical stoppage of cyclical decline after stage

TABLE 16

Commodity Groups in Order of Absolute Magnitudes of Price and Quantity Contributions to Joint Cyclical Variability

QUANTITY VARIABILITY		PRICE VARIABILITY	
Metals	2,731	Crop products, domestic	851
Durable goods	2,389	Producer goods for human	
Capital equipment	2,182	consumption	833
Other than American farm		Raw materials	801
products	1,418	Producer goods, all	656
Nonmetallic minerals	917	Nondurable goods	636
Producer goods, all	784	Human consumption goods	628
Manufactured goods	557	American farm products	622
All commodities	*435*	*All commodities*	*570*
Raw materials	354	Metals	542
Producer goods for human		Other than American farm	
consumption	297	products	531
Human consumption goods	177	Animal products, domestic	515
Consumer goods	88	Capital equipment	482
Nondurable goods	88	Foods	451
Animal products, domestic	55	Durable goods	444
American farm products	43	Nonmetallic minerals	428
Crop products, domestic	36	Manufactured goods	383
Foods	19	Consumer goods	357

VIII, contributes to this condition. This same condition, greater absolute variability of physical quantities during phases of reference expansion, is found among the various commodity groups, except goods for human consumption and the smaller group of foods.[16] The reverse is true, without a single exception, of prices. Mutable prices are an outstanding feature of business contractions. The divergence of prices from the cyclical average was distinctly more marked during contractions than during expansions, in the period covered by these records. [17] (Secular forces make some contribution to this result, in the present sample.)

[16] The difference between the figures for expansion and contraction is small for consumption goods and capital equipment. The present statement is based upon measures carried to a first decimal place.

[17] This evidence, which suggests that the quantity factor is a dominant lifter during business expansions, and that the price factor is a major depressant during business contractions, should be supplemented by more comprehensive observations. The severe contractions of 1920-21 and of 1929-33 are fairly heavily weighted in this sample, but the same relations prevail, for many commodities, in other reference cycles. We should note that for both quantities and prices the effects of secular factors are intertwined with those of cyclical forces.

From the average patterns of price-quantity behavior in reference cycles, measures of the elasticity of quantities and of the flexibility of unit prices have been derived for major commodity groups (Table 17). All the group measures for the full

TABLE 17

Commodity Groups in Order of Elasticity of Quantities and, Inversely, in Order of Flexibility of Prices in Business Cycles

| | PHASE MEASURES, ELASTICITY | | FULL CYCLE MEASURES | |
	Expansion	Contraction	Elasticity	Flexibility
Durable goods	+2.49	+2.18	+2.34	+0.43
Capital equipment	+2.59	+2.01	+2.30	+0.43
Metals	+2.29	+2.24	+2.26	+0.44
Other than American farm products	+1.92	+1.46	+1.69	+0.59
Nonmetallic minerals	+1.71	+1.15	+1.43	+0.70
Manufactured goods	+1.73	+1.08	+1.40	+0.71
Producer goods, all	+1.41	+0.98	+1.20	+0.83
All commodities	*+1.25*	*+0.81*	*+1.01*[a]	*+0.99*
Raw materials	+0.89	+0.61	+0.75	+1.33
Producer goods for human consumption	+0.93	+0.55	+0.74	+1.35
Human consumption goods	+0.85	+0.49	+0.67	+1.49
Consumer goods	+0.84	+0.38	+0.61	+1.64
Nondurable goods	+0.63	+0.28	+0.46	+2.17
Animal products, domestic	+0.51	+0.29	+0.40	+2.50
American farm products	+0.42	+0.22	+0.32	+3.12
Crop products, domestic	+0.34	+0.16	+0.25	+4.00
Foods	+0.14	—0.11	+0.02	+50.00

[a] See note to Table 12.

cycle are positive, an indication that within the framework of reference cycles forces related to business cycles are more powerful in determining price and quantity movements than are the narrower market influences that work toward inverse relations. The ranges are extensive, however—from 0.02 to 2.34 for e (from 50 to 0.43 for f). Perhaps no observations so far reviewed provide more impressive evidence concerning the diversity of market behavior patterns in business cycles. Quantities are most elastic (and prices least flexible) for durable goods, goods intended for use in capital equipment and building, minerals, manufactured goods, and producer goods—a showing quite in accord with expectation, and with evidence previously reviewed. For these goods, physical quantities change from 1.20 percent (producer goods) to 2.34 percent (durable goods) for every 1 percent change in price during business cycles. However, 9 of the 16 major commodity groups are marked by flexible prices (i.e., the coefficient f exceeds unity). Foods, farm products, nondurables generally, consumption goods, and raw materials are all of this type. For these goods prices change from 1.33 percent (raw materials) to 50 percent (foods) for every 1 percent change in quantities.

The elasticity measures for expansion and contraction are positive for all groups, except foods, for which quantities show a small net increase during business contractions, while prices drop. Among all other groups, as we pass from expansion to contraction, we find the decline in (positive) elasticity of quantities and the increase in (positive) flexibility of prices remarked in the all commodities pattern. It is generally characteristic of commodity markets that the responsiveness of quantities, viewed in relation to prices, is greater during general business expansion than during contraction; for prices relative responsiveness is greater during contraction.[18]

In Table 17 we have not set up the commodity groups in combinations corresponding to the original classifications, but the reader may find it interesting to do so. Sharp differences of behavior would be brought out thereby. With respect to prices in full cycles, raw materials are flexible (i.e., f is greater than 1), manufactured goods inflexible; farm products are flexible, nonfarm products inflexible; consumer goods are flexible, producer goods inflexible; goods for human consumption are flexible, capital goods inflexible; nondurable goods are flexible, durable goods highly inflexible. The observed differences accord with generally familiar evidence, but these measures give desirable precision to the record.

[18] The restricted meaning of measures of elasticity and flexibility derived from reference cycle relatives is to be emphasized. Price or quantity fluctuations that are not synchronized with cycles in general business will be dampened or eliminated when the reference cycle frame is imposed; the coefficients e and f will be correspondingly affected. To supplement the reference cycle record the fluctuations of physical quantities must be studied within a frame provided by specific cycles in the prices of individual commodities, and the fluctuations of commodity prices must be studied within a frame provided by specific cycles in the corresponding physical quantity series. Coefficients based on these additional studies will appear in a later report.

⊰ CHAPTER 4 ⊱

PATTERNS OF OUTLAY AND REVENUE:
AGGREGATIVE RECORD

IN Chapter 1 attention was given to recent cyclical fluctuations in gross national product. We now undertake a more intensive study of the monetary outlays of buyers (and the monetary receipts of sellers) in a somewhat more restricted sphere. We trace fluctuations in aggregate payments for a sample group of commodities which includes about one-third, by value, of total goods exchanged in the United States. From it we may learn something about the characteristics of cyclical fluctuations in the monetary outlays of buyers and about the relative importance, as factors in outlay variations, of changes in price and in the physical volume of goods traded.

The general cyclical patterns of buyers' outlays (i.e., aggregate values), average unit prices, and physical quantities are defined by the measures in Table 18, and are plotted in Chart 5. The movements of buyers' outlays conform closely to the movements of business at large during reference cycles, rising from a low at stage I to a peak at stage V, and falling to a low at stages VIII and IX. These monetary values have a range of

TABLE 18

Average Movements of Aggregate Values, Average Unit Prices,
and Physical Volume in Business Cycles, All Commodities

STAGE MEASURES
Reference Cycle Stages

	I	II	III	IV	V	VI	VII	VIII	IX
Value	85	97	105	118	125	116	99	85	85
Price	94	99	104	110	112	110	99	91	90
Quantity	90	98	101	108	112	107	99	94	94

	PHASE MEASURES, AVERAGE CHANGE		FULL CYCLE MEASURE
	Expansion	Contraction	Average Amplitude
Value	+40	—40	+80
Price	+18	—22	+40
Quantity	+22	—18	+40

These averages for all commodities are derived from stage averages defining price, quantity, and value patterns for 64 individual commodities. Stage averages for individual commodities are given equal weight in the derivation of the general averages in Table 18.

fluctuation during business cycles materially wider than that of average unit prices or physical quantities. For the commodities here studied, the amplitude of the cyclical swings in aggregate buyers' outlays is measured by an index of 80 (see the last column of Table 18). This signifies a fluctuation, from the

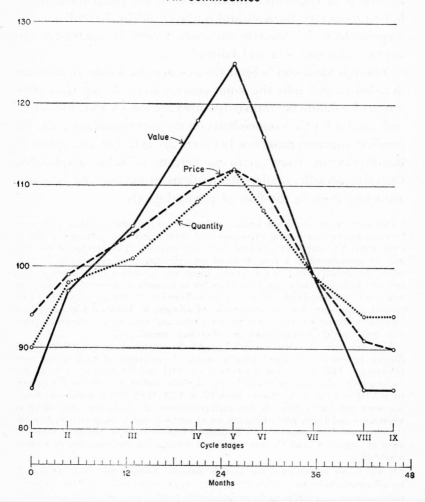

CHART 5

Average Movements of Unit Price, Physical Quantity, and Aggregate Buyers' Outlay in Business Cycles

All Commodities

trough of the cycle to the peak and back to the trough again, over a range equal to about 40 percent of the cycle average.[1] Price variations are about one-half as wide, some 20 percent of the cycle average; quantities have about the same amplitude as prices.[2] Cyclical variations in unit prices and in physical output, when averaged as they are in Table 18, are generally concurrent and in the same direction. They thus reenforce one another, and contribute to variations in monetary commitments (and in monetary payments) substantially wider than the variations in quantities. Business cycles are particularly manifest in monetary incomes and outlays, and in the dollar value accounts by which business enterprise records its operations and appraises its successes and failures.

There is variation behind the averages in Table 18, but the detailed record tells the same general story. If for each commodity we define the ratio of quantity amplitude to value amplitude, and array the commodities on the corresponding scale, the heaviest concentration lies between .50 and .70; i.e., quantity amplitudes are from 50 to 70 percent of value amplitudes. Characteristically, cyclical fluctuations in outlays and revenues are wider than in the flow of physical goods.

[1] The measure of amplitude employed in this study is the algebraic difference between movements during expansion and contraction (i.e., between reference cycle stages I-V and V-IX), in reference cycle relatives. The average of the two may be interpreted as a percentage of the reference cycle average for a given series. As already noted, if the specific highs and lows of a given series do not coincide with the highs and lows of cycles in business at large, the measure of 'reference cycle amplitude' of that series will understate the actual extent of its cyclical movements. For the three series of averages in Table 18 highs and lows coincide with, or are very close to, the peaks and troughs of reference cycles. The 'reference cycle amplitudes' are, therefore, meaningful.

The measures of reference cycle amplitude employed in general National Bureau procedure are based on the stages characteristic of each series' own movements. Thus if the low comes at stage VIII and the high at stage IV for a given series, the amplitude will be the algebraic difference between the change from VIII to IV and the change from IV to VIII. With this flexibility in locating lows and highs there is less understatement of amplitude than there is when lows and highs are arbitrarily set at stages I and V, respectively. But for the purposes of the present study a standard framework, with points of measurement at stages I, V, and IX, was considered desirable in the definition of cyclical amplitudes.

[2] If war cycles are omitted the average measures of reference cycle amplitude for all commodities are modified: value, 77; price, 34; quantity, 43. The quantity factor is some 25 percent again as variable as price, under peacetime conditions.

Rates of Change in Buyers' Outlays

The general direction of movement of buyers' outlays (and of sellers' revenues) during cycles in general business is shown in Chart 5 and Table 18. But how rapidly is the current flowing during the several stages of expansion? With the setting-in of contraction after stage V, how rapid is the ebb, and how do the rates of decline compare with the rates of advance? In answering these questions we use measures of interstage changes, expressed in terms of monthly rates (see Table 19).

TABLE 19

Average Monthly Interstage Changes in Prices, Quantities, and Values in Business Cycles, All Commodities

INTERSTAGE PERIOD	PRICE	QUANTITY	VALUE
I-II	+1.1	+1.7	+2.5
II-III	+0.6	+0.4	+0.9
III-IV	+0.7	+0.9	+1.6
IV-V	+0.6	+0.9	+1.6
V-VI	—0.7	—1.6	—2.5
VI-VII	—1.6	—1.1	—2.7
VII-VIII	—1.3	—0.9	—2.0
VIII-IX	—0.3	+0.1	—0.2

The unit is 1 percent of the average reference cycle standing of a given series. For an explanation of the derivation of average interstage changes see the footnote to Table 11.

In the terminal period of contraction, between stages VIII and IX of reference cycles, buyers' outlays decline slightly, as a result of a minor drop in average unit prices that more than offsets a very slight advance in quantities.[3] The turn in this aggregate tide after stage IX is sharp. The maximum rate of advance (2.5 per month) is recorded during the first period of recovery, between stages I and II. There is a sharp check during the next period (between stages II and III), but the advance continues. The current speeds up between stages III and V, but does not attain the earlier rate. The rise in outlays continues at a relatively high rate to the peak of activity in business at large, with no pause comparable to the almost com-

---

[3] Apparent minor discrepancies between Tables 18 and 19 are due to the fact that the entries in Table 18 are rounded to the nearest whole number while those in Table 19 are based upon figures carried to one decimal place.

plete immobility of the final period of contraction. The transition from expansion to contraction is therefore sharper. The rate of decline in the first two periods of contraction is high, the maximum rate occurring between stages VI and VII. The general picture is of recession in monetary payments for goods that moves steadily and with no great accelerations or retardations between stages V and VIII. The ebb of the tide in buyers' outlays is more concentrated and more uniform than the flow. At its maximum (2.7) the rate of decline is somewhat greater than the maximum rate of advance (2.5).[4]

The rates of change in the two component factors, which in all except the terminal period are lower than the rates for the total value series, were compared in the preceding chapter. We noted the narrow range of movements in the final period of contraction; the maximum rates of advance, for both unit prices and quantities, during interstage period I-II; the pronounced retardation of both between stages II and III; the maximum rate of decline in physical quantities during the first period of contraction, between stages V and VI, and the steady tapering off thereafter; the maximum rate of decline for unit prices between stages VI and VII; the excess of rates of fall in prices over those in quantities in all periods of contraction after stage VI.[5]

The amplitudes of the cyclical swings of prices and quantities, as averaged for all commodities, are about equal, and the stages at which cyclical lows and highs are recorded are nearly the same. However, the behavior of these two factors is far from the same during the expansion and contraction phases of business cycles. In the first rush of recovery and during the stages when prosperity is in full bloom rates of advance in quantities exceed those in prices. When the turn is rounded,

---

[4] The rate of decline in buyers' outlays appears to be at its maximum in the first period of contraction (between stages V and VI) when war cycles are omitted. But the records including and excluding war cycles show substantially the same sequences and relations.

[5] It will be understood that these statements relate to the particular sample studied. The final condition noted (excess of rates of fall in prices over those in quantities in all periods of contraction after stage VI) probably reflects the fairly heavy weight given to agricultural products in this sample. (Prices of farm products are subject to a notable weakening after stage VI.) The relationship observed is not generally true of industrial products.

and contraction sets in, quantities drop more sharply at first. Thereafter, prices are the chief bearish factor, in the over-all record of Table 19.

Scope of Expansions and Contractions in Buyers' Outlays

Measures of the average standing of buyers' outlays and of corresponding unit price and quantity series fail to define actual conditions in commodity markets during business cycles, in all their complexity. For there are innumerable cross-currents in these markets. Buyers' outlays may be increasing for some commodities while they are declining for others. Behind these diverse movements of monetary payments are still more diverse combinations of related price and quantity changes. We may get at some of these, from the value side, by studying the extent to which commodities participate in the general advances and declines of aggregate outlays during business cycles, and in the different phases of business cycles. We seek, that is, to determine the degree to which fluctuations in the stream of monetary payments for commodities accord with the general tides of business expansion and contraction.

Reference cycles, it will be recalled, are divided into nine stages, I to V covering expansion, V to IX, contraction. Observations on our 64 commodities cover, in all, 4,160 interstage movements of commodity values (the unit of observation is the change in the value of a single commodity between two stages, e.g., from II to III, of a given reference cycle). The complete record shown in the accompanying summary of the movements of monetary payments for commodities, in successive stages of

	INTERSTAGE CHANGES	
	Number	Percent
Movements of values in full cycle		
With cyclical tide	2,791	67
Against cyclical tide	1,369	33
Total	4,160	100

business cycles, reveals a fairly high degree of concordance between changes in commodity values and the prevailing tides of business. Approximately two-thirds of all interstage changes in commodity values are in the same direction as the cyclical movement of general business; about one-third run counter to it. In indicating the mixed character of cyclical movements, these figures give a just picture of business cycles. Conflicting currents and countermovements are always present;[6] the cyclical swings of business reflect preponderant tendencies toward expansion or contraction, never complete uniformity of movement in one direction.[7]

When we pass from the record for the full cycle to separate phases of expansion and contraction, we note some variation in the relative importance of the contracyclical currents. For

	INTERSTAGE CHANGES	
	Number	Percent
Movements of values		
During expansions		
With cyclical tide	1,460	70
Against cyclical tide	620	30
Total	2,080	100
During contractions		
With cyclical tide	1,331	64
Against cyclical tide	749	36
Total	2,080	100

[6] Not all the countermovements represent changes conflicting with the currents of business cycles. Cyclical forces themselves generate some nonconforming movements—leads, lags, and inversions.

[7] If we take as the unit of observation not the movement of values for one commodity between two successive stages of a given reference cycle but the movement of values for a single commodity between two successive stages of the average pattern for that commodity (as exemplified by pig iron in Chart 1) we reduce markedly the aberrant behavior behind the pattern for a single commodity. With primary interest attaching to the typical behavior of individual commodities it is desirable, indeed, to ignore the idiosyncrasies of individual reference cycles and concentrate on the average pattern characteristic of each commodity. On this basis we have observations on average patterns for 64 commodities, each pattern comprehending 8 interstage periods—a total of 512 observations, divided as in the accompanying tabulation. Here the agreement between changes in commodity values and the prevailing tides of business is higher. More than three-quarters of the interstage changes in average value patterns are with the cyclical movements of business at large. The removal of aberrations in individual reference cycles reveals typical changes in buyers' outlays for individual commodities conforming in high degree to the pattern of reference cycles.

	INTERSTAGE CHANGES	
	Number	Percent
Movements, in full cycle, of values defined		
in average patterns		
With cyclical tide	394	77
Against cyclical tide	118	23
Total	512	100

the 4,160 observations cyclical expansion is marked by a movement of buyers' outlays somewhat stronger and more uniform than that found in contraction. During expansion values move with the cyclical tide in 70 percent of all interstage changes; during contraction only 64 percent move with the tide. The larger proportion of aberrant movements during contraction doubtless reflects the influence of the rising secular trend in physical volume characteristic of most of the period covered by these observations. This movement, which apparently outweighs the declining trend in unit prices, would tend to diminish the intensity of contractions, and to enhance the intensity of expansions.[8]

The ebbs and flows of the stream of monetary payments during business cycles may be studied in greater detail in the records for interstage periods—four in expansion, four in contraction. Relevant evidence bearing on variations, from stage to stage of expansion and from stage to stage of contraction, in the intensity and uniformity of the flow of payments for commodities is summarized in Table 20 and is presented graphically in Chart 6. Table and chart are based on average outlay patterns for the commodities studied. In this summary, therefore, we are working with typical or characteristic modes of cyclical behavior of individual commodities, abstracting from the variations that occur from cycle to cycle.

Changes in the outlays of buyers (and in the revenues of sellers) are predominantly positive between stages I and V of refer-

---

[8] When attention is concentrated on the average patterns for the 64 commodities studied, the same general relations are found. Conformity of outlays, as defined by average patterns, is high in both expansion and contraction, but somewhat higher in the former.

	INTERSTAGE CHANGES	
	Number	Percent
Movements of values defined in average patterns		
During expansions		
With cyclical tide	203½	79
Against cyclical tide	52½	21
Total	256	100
During contractions		
With cyclical tide	190½	74
Against cyclical tide	65½	26
Total	256	100

TABLE 20

Changes in Proportions of Commodities for Which Buyers' Outlays
Increase and Decrease between Successive Stages of Business Cycles

	INTERSTAGE				PERIOD		
	I- II	II- III	III- IV	IV- V	V- VI	VI- VII	VII- VIII	VIII- IX

	I-II	II-III	III-IV	IV-V	V-VI	VI-VII	VII-VIII	VIII-IX
Percentage of commodities for which outlays:								
increase (value changes are positive)	84	64	89	80	23	16	17	45
decrease (value changes are negative)	16	36	11	20	77	84	83	55

The base of the two percentages given for each interstage period is 64.

ence cycles, predominantly negative between stages V and IX, but mixed movements occur at all stages. The proportion of all transactions involving increases in the monetary outlays of buyers is at a minimum between stages VI and VIII. Forces making for contraction dominate markets at this time; the tide of business is ebbing most strongly. Yet even in this period about one-sixth of all changes in the monetary values of goods are positive. In some markets buyers are increasing their outlays; the receipts of sellers are expanding. In the final phase of general contraction, when business at large is at its lowest point, positive value changes amount to 45 percent of the total. The tide is still ebbing—55 percent of all value changes are negative—but the forces of recovery in the markets for commodities are almost strong enough to offset the negative factors.

When stage IX (which coincides with stage I) has been passed, the tide is running strongly toward recovery. Between stages I and II, 84 percent of all changes in monetary outlays for commodities are positive. Some declines persist—16 percent of the total—but forces making for expansion dominate commodity markets at large. In the next period, between stages II and III of reference cycles, a check occurs; positive outlay changes fall to 64 percent of the total; declines constitute 36 percent. This retardation, coming after the first sharp spurt of recovery, is a characteristic and persistent feature of business cycles, observable over a wide range of economic processes.[9]

[9] See the forthcoming monograph by Wesley C. Mitchell, *What Happens during Business Cycles: A Progress Report* (National Bureau of Economic Research).

CHART 6

Changes in Outlays for Commodities by Stages of Business Cycles

Proportions of all commodities for which buyers' outlays increase
and decrease between successive cyclical stages

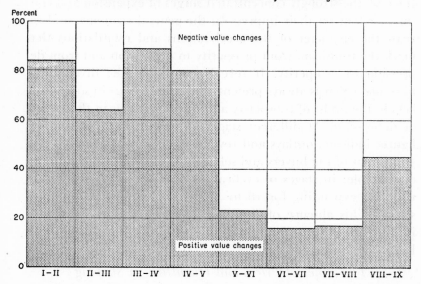

Between stages III and IV the stream of monetary payments
again swells. Of all outlay changes 89 percent are positive, 11
percent negative. Indeed, at this period the stream of monetary
payments is running more uniformly in one direction than it
is at any other cyclical period. As stage IV is passed, the forces
of recession gain strength. The percentage of positive value
changes drops to 80 between stages IV and V; the percentage
of negative changes rises to 20. With the general turn of the
tide at stage V, 57 percent of all outlay changes shift from the
positive to the negative column, and the percentage of negative
value changes rises to 77. Thereafter the extent of participation
in the contraction rises, reaching a maximum between stages
VI and VIII when buyers' outlays are declining for about five-
sixths of all commodities. In the final period of general contraction this proportion falls to slightly more than one-half
(55 percent).

The record of buyers' outlays set forth above has deficiencies in both coverage and accuracy, but it represents with reasonable faithfulness the changing aggregate of monetary payments for major classes of commodities as business cycles run their course. It shows the strongly concentrated surges of expansion and contraction that set their impress on the general economy, and reveals the character of the accelerations and retardations that mark the transition from prosperity to depression and from depression to prosperity. It reveals, moreover, the diversity of movement that is always present—the contractions in some markets in the midst of prosperity and the expansions in the depths of depression. At different stages of cyclical expansion, these figures indicate, outlays and revenues are contracting for 11 to 36 percent of the buyers and sellers of commodities included in our sample; in stages of cyclical contraction outlays and revenues are expanding for 16 to 45 percent of these buyers and sellers. This absence of complete uniformity of movement is in both its aspects an element of stability in the economy at large.

The Roles of Prices and Quantities in Shaping the Movements of Monetary Payments for Commodities

The outlays of buyers and the revenues of sellers may change because of alterations in the physical quantities of goods being exchanged, or because of alterations in average unit prices. The average patterns of behavior of these two factors have been noted (see Chart 5 and Table 18) and the relation of their rates of change to changes in buyers' outlays has been examined (see Table 19). We seek now to trace in greater detail the parts played by changes in quantities and in average unit prices in the cyclical movements of commodity values. Which is the dominant factor in determining the cyclical fluctuations in outlays and revenues? Which is the more important in expansions? In contractions? Which is dominant at each stage of expansion and contraction?

For the over-all record we use 4,160 cases of interstage change in commodity values, a majority being movements with the cyclical tide, a strong minority running counter to the current. In 58 percent of the recorded movements the quantity factor

	NO. OF INTERSTAGE CHANGES	PERCENTAGE IN WHICH	
		Price is dominant	Quantity is dominant
Movements of values in full cycle			
With cyclical tide	2,791	44	56
Against cyclical tide	1,369	39	61
Total	4,160	42	58

was the chief determinant of the direction and amount of the observed change in value; changes in unit prices were dominant in 42 percent of the cases. Both factors contributed, but changes in the quantities of goods exchanged were chiefly responsible for the expansions and contractions in monetary outlays during business cycles. This evidence, which is straightforward and detailed, is of considerable importance. Comparison of the relative amplitudes of price and of quantity cycles, of relative rates of change in averages of the two factors, of the extent of participation of prices and quantities in the cyclical movements of general business are all somewhat indirect and equivocal in their bearing on the central question here at issue: Are changes in prices or in quantities chiefly responsible for cyclical expansions and contractions in the stream of monetary payments for commodities? The full count of individual cases, period by period of reference cycles, shows a clear predominance of the quantity factor.[10]

In investigating the character of the influence exerted by each factor this general count may be analyzed in various ways. We have seen that about two-thirds of all changes in the monetary values of the commodities here studied were movements with the cyclical tide of general business; one-third were against the tide. Quantity is dominant in shaping both movements, but its influence is distinctly stronger in determining the value changes that reverse the cyclical tide. Here the percentage of quantity dominance is 61 as against 56 for quantity dominance in value movements conforming to cycles in general business.

For further light on these movements we study the separate phases of expansion and contraction. The relative dominance

---

[10] When the count is made on the basis of *average* patterns for individual commodities, we find that the quantity factor is dominant in 60 percent of interstage changes in outlay, price in 40 percent.

	NO. OF INTERSTAGE CHANGES	PERCENTAGE IN WHICH Price is dominant	Quantity is dominant
Movements of values			
During expansions			
With cyclical tide	1,460	41	59
Against cyclical tide	620	42	58
Total	2,080	42	58
During contractions			
With cyclical tide	1,331	46	54
Against cyclical tide	749	36	64
Total	2,080	43	57

of the quantity factor is substantially the same in the two phases, but there are appreciable differences when changes in value that accord with the cyclical tide are distinguished from changes countering the tide. Quantity movements are most important, relatively, when they are pushing values upward against an ebbing cyclical tide. Prices exert their greatest influence when they are pushing values downward with an ebbing cyclical tide. The record in this respect is the same whether we include the full count of value changes in separate reference cycles or concentrate on patterns of average behavior of individual commodities. Both counts agree, moreover, in indicating the preponderant influence of quantity in determining value changes.

We probe more deeply into these processes by examining the roles of price and quantity factors in shaping the movements of monetary outlays at successive stages of expansion and contraction. Here we shall deal with the average behavior of individual commodities. For each interstage period we have a record of the average change in buyers' outlays for each of 64 commodities. These are summarized in Table 21, and shown graphically in Chart 7.

We may start with the interstage period VII-VIII, when only 11 of the 64 commodities included show positive value changes in their average outlay patterns. Increases in the quantities of goods exchanged account for all positive value changes. At this stage of contraction, when the tide is ebbing strongly, pick-ups in physical volume are responsible for all observed expansions in monetary payments for commodities as these are reflected in average outlay patterns for individual goods.[11]

---

11 If we go behind the averages to detailed commodity records, cycle by cycle, we find less uniformity, but the quantity factor is still dominant.

TABLE 21

Value Changes by Reference Cycle Stages
Roles of Price and Quantity Factors

	INTERSTAGE PERIOD							
	I-II	II-III	III-IV	IV-V	V-VI	VI-VII	VII-VIII	VIII-IX
POSITIVE VALUE CHANGES								
Number	54	41	57	51½	15	10½	11	29
Percentage in which								
Price is dominant	41	43	42	40	53	17	0	21
Quantity is dominant	59	57	58	60	47	83	100	79
NEGATIVE VALUE CHANGES								
Number	10	23	7	12½	49	53½	53	35
Percentage in which								
Price is dominant	45	24	43	32	37	47	55	39
Quantity is dominant	55	76	57	68	63	53	45	61

For each interstage period there are 64 observations. Each observation defines the change in buyers' outlays for a single commodity during that period as averaged for all the business cycles covered by the value series for that commodity.

The entries in Table 21, and in the similar tables following, are based upon comparisons of average monthly rates of change in the prices, quantities, and monetary values of individual commodities. The rates of change for each commodity are unweighted averages of the monthly rates, by interstage periods, for all the reference cycles covered by the records for that commodity. That is, in getting an average rate of change in the price of a given commodity between reference cycle stages III and IV, for example, we average, with equal weights, rates for that interstage period in all the reference cycles covered. No attempt is made to weight on the basis of duration. For the present purpose we assume that a monthly rate-of-change observation for an interstage period lasting four months is as important as a monthly rate-of-change observation for the same period (in another cycle) lasting twelve months. The reference cycle is the unit of measurement, and all reference cycles are assumed to be of equal weight.

For consistency with such graphic presentations as that given in Chart 1, in the derivation of which account is taken of interstage durations, weights based on duration should be used in the computation of average rates of change. Both weighted and unweighted average rates will be given by the National Bureau in publishing basic cycle records.

Between stages VIII and IX, the final period of general business contraction, the number of positive changes among buyers' outlays increases substantially. The quantity factor accounts for 79 percent of these, prices for 21 percent. In the next four interstage periods, between stages I and V of the reference expansion, the role of quantities remains predominant. Approximately three-fifths of all increases in buyers' outlays are chiefly due to increases in the number of units exchanged, approximately two-fifths to price increases. With the passing of the peak in general business activity at stage V the number of value increases falls sharply, and there is a reversal of the relative strengths of prices and quantities as positive factors. Price accounts for slightly more than half of the few outlay increases between stages V and VI. After stage VI the positive influence of prices declines sharply, reaching its minimum between stages VII and VIII.

The roles of prices and quantities as factors contributing to increases in the outlays of buyers and the revenues of sellers are shown graphically in Chart 7. This reveals the dominant role of quantities in all interstage periods except V-VI; the high importance of quantity increases in the terminal stages of contraction; the relative constancy of the two factors during the entire reference expansion; the sharp drop in the positive influence of prices after stage VI when general contraction is characteristic of the economy.

The series measuring the number of decreases in buyers' outlays for goods (i.e., the negative value changes in Table 21) runs inversely to that measuring the number of increases, but the roles of price and quantity as factors in the decreases and the increases are quite different. Prices are pressing downward most strongly between stages VI and VIII of contraction, particularly between stages VII and VIII. These are the periods, it will be recalled, when the influence of price as a factor making for increases in monetary payments is at a minimum. When the full tide of contraction is running, prices are going with the current and doing little to check or reverse it. In its influence on buyers' outlays the quantity factor is dominant negatively in all except one (VII-VIII) interstage period, as it is dominant positively in all except one (V-VI). There is, however, considerable variation in the strength of the downward push exerted by physical quantities. They are strongest, relatively, in the check to expansion that comes after stage II and in the turn of the cyclical tide between stages IV and VI. The marked retardation of recovery after stage II and the first sweep of recession are primarily physical phenomena. The negative influence of price is at its lowest in these periods.

CHART 7

Relative Importance of Price and Quantity Factors in Determining the Proportion of Commodities for which Buyers' Outlays Increase and Decrease, from Stage to Stage of Business Cycles

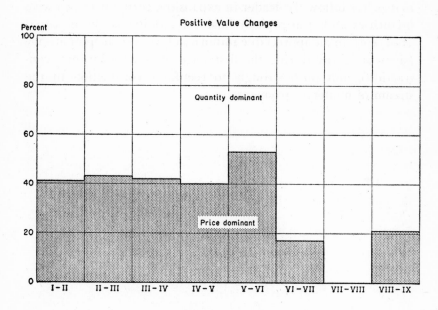

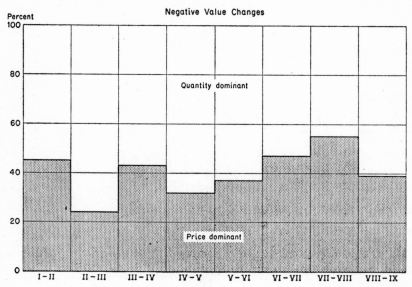

In summary, the evidence we have here examined indicates that physical expansion is the dominant factor in the reversal of cyclical declines in buyers' outlays and sellers' revenues; that declines in physical quantity interrupt the general advance after stage II and play a leading role in the generation of recession; that prices follow the leader in expansion, turn downward with quantities after the peak of business activity has been passed (but work in an appreciable minority of cases to keep monetary payments rising during the first stage of general business contraction), and push strongly to reenforce contraction in the stream of monetary payments.

⟨ CHAPTER 5 ⟩

PATTERNS OF OUTLAY AND REVENUE:
BEHAVIOR OF COMMODITY GROUPS

IN Chapter 4 we have followed the swellings and contractions of the broad stream of buyers' outlays for commodities, during business cycles, and have attempted to determine the relative importance of changes in the physical volume of goods exchanged and in average unit prices as factors in the cyclical movements of aggregate outlay. This aggregate is made up of payments for goods of many varieties—raw and processed, farm and industrial, consumption and capital goods—and there is reason to believe that there are material differences among these varieties in the cyclical movements of buyers' outlays and in the roles of price and quantity factors in these movements. In surveying the behavior of these commodity groups we deal first with the cyclical patterns of buyers' outlays, then with the parts played by unit prices and physical volume as determinants of outlay movements.

Reference cycle patterns of buyers' outlays for 16 important categories of goods are given in Table 22 and are plotted in Chart 8.[1] The swings of monetary payments for these various kinds of goods are much the same in their timing and direction. Outlays for all classes reach their peak at stage V, when business at large is most active. The chief differences in timing relate to the final period of contraction. For 5 (overlapping) classes of goods—American farm products, crop products, consumer goods, foods, and nondurable goods generally—buyers' outlays begin to expand after stage VIII. Outlays for raw materials, animal products, and goods intended for human consumption remain at a constant level between stages VIII and IX. For all other groups the low point comes at stage IX, and revival of outlays coincides with the beginning of expansion in the economy at large. We shall have more to say later on the question of timing.

[1] See Appendix Table 2 and Ch. 3, note 13, for explanation of these commodity groups.

TABLE 22

Average Movements of Buyers' Outlays for Groups of Commodities in Business Cycles

	I	II	III	IV	V	VI	VII	VIII	IX
					REFERENCE CYCLE STAGES				
All commodities	85	97	105	118	125	116	99	85	85
Raw materials	85	97	104	118	127	118	99	86	86
Manufactured goods	86	97	106	117	124	113	98	85	84
American farm products	94	103	105	115	119	112	97	89	91
Other than American farm products	77	91	104	121	132	121	100	81	79
Crop products, domestic	95	104	104	116	121	113	95	88	91
Animal products, domestic	93	102	105	114	117	111	99	90	90
Metals	70	89	106	127	140	124	99	77	72
Nonmetallic minerals	78	88	99	115	126	121	106	86	84
Producer goods, all	81	96	105	121	130	118	98	83	81
Producer goods for human consumption	87	99	106	120	127	117	97	86	85
Consumer goods	93	98	103	112	116	111	100	90	92
Capital equipment	75	92	106	125	138	123	98	79	75
Human consumption goods	89	99	105	116	123	115	99	87	87
Foods	96	101	104	112	113	109	100	93	96
Durable goods	73	90	106	125	137	123	99	78	74
Nondurable goods	91	100	104	115	120	113	98	89	90

More notable are the differences in amplitude (Table 23). The relative amplitudes of the cyclical swings in buyers' outlays for these types of goods reflect behavior characteristics that are now generally recognized. The outlays of buyers (and the revenues of sellers) are most variable for the products of heavy industry—metals, durable goods, capital equipment—which are traditionally susceptible to the forces of expansion and contraction. Near the bottom of the list are foods, consumer goods, farm products, and nondurable goods generally. The range of difference extends from an amplitude index of 34 for foods (representing cyclical variations of some 17 percent in expan-

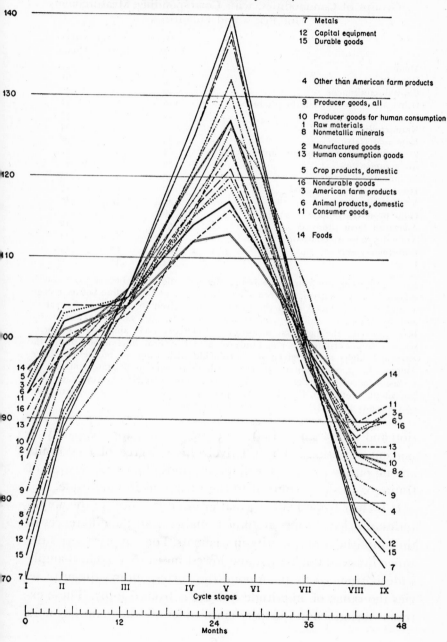

CHART 8

Average Movements of Buyers' Outlays in Business Cycles
Sixteen Major Commodity Groups

7   Metals
12 Capital equipment
15 Durable goods

4   Other than American farm products

9   Producer goods, all

10 Producer goods for human consumption
1   Raw materials
8   Nonmetallic minerals

2   Manufactured goods
13 Human consumption goods

5   Crop products, domestic

16 Nondurable goods
3   American farm products

6   Animal products, domestic
11 Consumer goods

14 Foods

Cycle stages

Months

TABLE 23

Amplitudes of Cyclical Fluctuations in Buyers' Outlays for
Groups of Commodities, with Corresponding Measurements
for Prices and Quantities

| | REFERENCE CYCLE AMPLITUDE | | |
	Value	Price	Quantity
Metals	138	43	97
Durable goods	127	39	91
Capital equipment	126	39	89
Other than American farm products	108	42	71
Producer goods, all	98	46	54
Nonmetallic minerals	90	37	54
Raw materials	83	49	36
Producer goods for human consumption	82	48	34
All commodities	*80*	*40*	*40*
Manufactured goods	78	33	45
Human consumption goods	70	42	27
Nondurable goods	59	42	18
Crop products, domestic	56	43	10
American farm products	53	40	12
Animal products, domestic	51	37	14
Consumer goods	47	30	17
Foods	34	33	0

Each group amplitude measure is the algebraic difference between the rise, in reference cycle relatives, between stages I and V and the decline between stages V and IX. It is based upon the stage averages given in Table 22 (for values) and in Appendix Table 3 (for prices, quantities, and values). Attention has been called to the fact that measures of 'reference cycle amplitude' for given series will understate the magnitude of actual cyclical fluctuations unless the lows and highs of the given series coincide with those of business at large. Among the present commodity groups there is some understatement for the 5 classes for which outlays reach their low points in reference cycle stage VIII. We should note, too, that the method of averaging necessarily dampens non-synchronous fluctuations of individual components.

sion and 17 in contraction) to 138 for metals (approximately 69 percent variation). The relatively high degree of conformity among outlay patterns for different kinds of goods in respect of timing is in sharp contrast to the variations in amplitude.

It is clear from Table 23 that group differences in the amplitudes of price changes are much smaller than the differences in the amplitudes of quantity movements. For the price series the range between the highest and lowest measure of cyclical amplitude is from 30 to 49. Among the corresponding quantity series the range of amplitude indexes is from 0 to 97. These extreme variations in quantity amplitudes are the main factor in the widely varying value amplitudes. This showing confirms other evidence indicating that the ties among prices are closer than among quantities, that commodity prices respond more uniformly than do physical quantities to cyclical forces. This generalization holds when we deal with individual commodities in an undifferentiated aggregate; it is equally true when commodities are classified on the basis of their origin, use, durability, or standing in the productive-distributive process. Within these major groups, as between them, fluctuations in prices are more uniform than those in quantities, in the amplitude of their movements.

Intensity of Outlay Changes

The rate of increase in buyers' outlays for commodities in general, we have seen, was at its maximum between stages I and II of reference cycles; the rate of decline was highest between stages VI and VII (Table 19). The record for commodity groups is given in Table 24. The groups are here listed in the order of the timing, within the reference cycle, of their maximum rates of increase in value. For one group, foods, the rate of increase in buyers' outlays is highest between stages VIII and IX, the terminal period of general business contraction. For 13 groups increase in outlays is at its maximum between stages I and II of reference cycles. Outlays for consumer goods are advancing most rapidly between stages III and IV.[2] One group, nonmetallic minerals, reaches its highest rate of advance in the final phase of general expansion, between reference cycle stages IV and V. The differences among the maximum rates correspond, in general, to the differences in amplitude, with the heavier, durable, producer goods classes having the highest maxima. The early advance in aggregate expenditures for foods and the attainment of maximum outlay increases for consumer goods and nonmetallic minerals midway or late in expansion are notable departures from the pattern of general group behavior.

[2] This does not necessarily mean that the outlays of final consumers are advancing most rapidly during this period. The quantity records and price quotations used here are for quantity movements and prices at distributive stages preceding retailing operations.

TABLE 24

Periods of Maximum Monthly Rates of Increase in Buyers' Outlays for Groups of Commodities, with Corresponding Measurements for Prices and Quantities

	INTERSTAGE PERIOD	AV. MONTHLY RATE OF CHANGE Value	Price	Quantity
Foods	VIII-IX	+1.3	+0.4	+0.8*
Metals	I-II	+3.6	+0.7	+3.5*
Capital equipment	I-II	+3.5	+0.7	+3.1*
Durable goods	I-II	+3.5	+0.7	+3.1*
Producer goods, all	I-II	+3.2	+1.2*	+2.1*
Other than American farm products	I-II	+3.0	+0.8	+2.5*
Producer goods for human consumption	I-II	+2.9	+1.5*	+1.4*
Raw materials	I-II	+2.7	+1.3*	+1.5*
All commodities	*I-II*	*+2.5*	*+1.0**	*+1.6**
Manufactured goods	I-II	+2.2	+0.6*a	+1.7*
Human consumption goods	I-II	+2.1	+1.0*	+1.1*
American farm products	I-II	+2.0	+1.1*	+0.7*b
Animal products, domestic	I-II	+2.0	+0.9*	+1.0*
Crop products, domestic	I-II	+2.0	+1.5*	+0.2
Nondurable goods	I-II	+2.0	+1.1*	+0.9*
Consumer goods	III-IV	+1.3	+0.4	+0.7
Nonmetallic minerals	IV-V	+2.8	+1.0*	+1.8*

In deriving rates of change for commodity groups, average monthly rates by interstage periods for all the commodities in each group have been averaged, the measures for individual commodities being equally weighted. This is consistent with the method of deriving the average monthly rates for individual commodities (see note to Table 21). The average rates for 'all commodities' given in Tables 24 and 25 and in the related footnotes have been similarly derived. It will be noted that these 'all commodity' rates differ slightly from those given in Tables 11 and 19, in the computation of which account was taken of the varying average durations of the different interstage periods (see note to Table 11).

* Maximum rate of advance.
a Same maximum rate of advance occurs during interstage period IV-V.
b Same maximum rate of advance occurs during interstage period III-IV.

Average rates of change in unit price and in quantity for the periods in which outlays advance at maximum rates are also shown in Table 24. For 12 of the 16 commodity groups the rates of increase in volume exceed the rates of increase in price. That is, the sharpest accelerations in outlays are attributable chiefly to increases in the physical volume of purchases. Only for farm products, crop products, producer goods for human consumption, and nondurable goods (categories comprehending many of the same products) are the rates of price increase higher than the rates of change in volume during the periods of maximum advance in buyers' outlays. These are, typically, goods the supply of which is not readily expansible under the pressure of increased demand.

In general, maximum rates of advance in prices and in quantities came, also, during the first period of general business expansion.[3] This was true, as regards prices, for 10 of the

[3] Periods of maximum rate of advance in price and quantity, for the various commodity groups here studied, are set forth below.

	INTERSTAGE PERIOD	AV. MONTHLY RISE IN PRICE
Crop products, domestic	I-II	+1.5
Producer goods for human consumption	I-II	+1.5
Raw materials	I-II	+1.3
Producer goods, all	I-II	+1.2
American farm products	I-II	+1.1
Nondurable goods	I-II	+1.1
All commodities	*I-II*	*+1.0*
Human consumption goods	I-II	+1.0
Animal products, domestic	I-II	+0.9
Foods	I-II	+0.7
Manufactured goods	I-II & IV-V	+0.6
Metals	IV-V	+1.1
Capital equipment	IV-V	+1.0
Durable goods	IV-V	+1.0
Nonmetallic minerals	IV-V	+1.0
Other than American farm products	IV-V	+1.0
Consumer goods	IV-V	+0.6

	INTERSTAGE PERIOD	AV. MONTHLY RISE IN QUANTITY
Consumer goods	VIII-IX	+0.9
Foods	VIII-IX	+0.8
Metals	I-II	+3.5
Capital equipment	I-II	+3.1
Durable goods	I-II	+3.1
Other than American farm products	I-II	+2.5
Producer goods, all	I-II	+2.1
Manufactured goods	I-II	+1.7
All commodities	*I-II*	*+1.6*
Raw materials	I-II	+1.5
Producer goods for human consumption	I-II	+1.4
Human consumption goods	I-II	+1.1
Animal products, domestic	I-II	+1.0
Nondurable goods	I-II	+0.9
American farm products	I-II & III-IV	+0.7
Crop products, domestic	III-IV	+0.8
Nonmetallic minerals	IV-V	+1.8

16 classes of goods. The other 6 groups all experienced their maximum price accelerations in the final period of business expansion, between stages IV and V. The goods thus lagging in their price response include metals and nonmetallic minerals, durables, capital equipment, and nonfarm products—commodities for which output can be readily expanded as the tide of business recovery first begins to flow. For these goods the pressures of demand on supply, that generate sharp price advances, come late in the recovery phase. Also among the products showing maximum price advance in the final phase of business expansion are consumer goods, which are marked by steady but modest advances during the entire reference expansion, with only slight variation from stage to stage.

Twelve of the 16 categories achieved their maximum rate of advance in physical quantities during the first period of reference expansion. Two groups—consumer goods and foods—registered maximum rates of advance in the preceding period, between stages VIII and IX of the reference cycle. For consumer goods and foods, that is, the upward movement of quantities was at its maximum during the terminal period of contraction in general business.[4] The strategic importance of this apparent recovery in the consumer segment of the economy, coming while contraction prevails in the economy at large, is clear.

We may follow the record of contraction in buyers' outlays in Table 25, in which the periods and rates of maximum decline are set forth by commodity groups. One outstanding feature of the table is that the rates of maximum decline in buyers' outlays are higher, for all except 2 of the 16 commodity groups, than the corresponding rates of maximum advance in Table 24. For nearly all classes of commodities the decline in

[4] The evidence of general index numbers on this point is conflicting. An index of the production of foodstuffs, constructed by the National Bureau and covering five recent cycles, confirms the present sample in showing the maximum rate of advance in interstage period VIII-IX. Two index numbers of the production of consumer goods (those of Leong and of the Federal Reserve Bank of New York) show declines in output in this period, but at low rates. A similar index of the Harvard Economic Service, covering three business cycles between 1919 and 1927, has its next to the highest rate of advance in the terminal period of general business contraction.

buyers' outlays during business contractions is sharper, more violent, more intense, than the rise during expansions. Only for animal products and foods is the reverse true, and for these the difference between the maximum rates of change in the two cyclical phases is slight.

The two phases differ, also, in the timing of the periods of maximum rates of change. Most commodity groups achieve their maximum advances in the first period of expansion (between stages I and II of reference cycles). Maximum declines come in the second period of general contraction (between stages VI and VII of reference cycles) for most groups. Manufactured goods, crop products, and farm products react promptly and sharply to recession, buyers' outlays

TABLE 25

Periods of Maximum Monthly Rates of Decrease in Buyers' Outlays for Groups of Commodities, with Corresponding Measurements for Prices and Quantities

	INTERSTAGE PERIOD	AV. MONTHLY RATE OF CHANGE		
		Value	Price	Quantity
Crop products, domestic	V-VI	—3.2	—1.3	—1.3*
Manufactured goods	V-VI	—2.7	—0.3	—2.2*
Nondurable goods	V-VI	—2.2	—0.7	—1.2*
	VI-VII	—2.2	—1.6*	—0.6
American farm products	V-VI	—2.1	—0.8	—1.0*
Foods	V-VI	—1.0	—0.3	—0.6*
	VI-VII	—1.0	—1.4*	+0.3
Metals	VI-VII	—4.6	—1.5*	—2.8
Capital equipment	VI-VII	—4.2	—1.5*	—2.5
Durable goods	VI-VII	—4.1	—1.4*	—2.5
Other than American farm products	VI-VII	—3.6	—1.3	—2.1
Producer goods, all	VI-VII	—3.4	—1.8*	—1.6
Raw materials	VI-VII	—3.3	—2.0*	—1.2*a
Producer goods for human consumption	VI-VII	—3.1	—2.0*	—1.1
All commodities	VI-VII	—2.8	—1.5*	—1.2
Human consumption goods	VI-VII	—2.4	—1.6*	—0.8
Animal products, domestic	VI-VII	—1.8	—1.3*b	—0.6
Nonmetallic minerals	VII-VIII	—3.6	—1.3*	—2.3*
Consumer goods	VII-VIII	—1.5	—1.3*	—0.3

* Maximum rate of decline.
a Same maximum rate of decline occurs during interstage period V-VI.
b Same maximum rate of decline occurs during interstage period VII-VIII.

dropping most rapidly between stages V and VI; consumer goods and nonmetallic minerals respond more slowly, outlays dropping most sharply between stages VII and VIII. But for nearly all commodities outlays turn downward after stage V, and fall with accelerated intensity between stages VI and VII. The decline is unbroken in the next period between stages VII and VIII, but at a slower tempo. It is significant that for no group is the decline in buyers' outlays at its maximum between stages VIII and IX, the terminal period of general business contraction.

The records of intensity of outlay changes during expansion and contraction differ significantly in the relative roles of quantities and prices. The quantity factor is dominant for 'all commodities' and in 12 of the 16 individual groups in contributing to maximum outlay changes in expansion (see Table 24). In contraction, price contributes more than quantity in the period (VI-VII) of maximum decline in buyers' outlays for commodities at large. For about half of the groups listed, price is the major contributor to outlay drops in the period of maximum decline; for the other half, and notably among manufactured goods, quantity provides the chief stimulus to declines. Taking account of all the commodities and groups here studied, it is clear that price has been more important as a factor reducing monetary outlays and revenues in periods of business contraction than as a factor in augmenting outlays and revenues in expansion.

Separate study of the price and quantity factors, by groups, with respect to the timing of their maximum rates of decline, reveals certain notable resemblances and differences between the stages of maximum advance and of maximum decline.[5] For all except one group the maximum rate of decline in quantity is attained in the first period of business contraction, between stages V and VI.[6] (Nonmetallic minerals, which lagged in their physical volume response to the forces of expansion, lag also in contraction, reaching their maximum rate of fall between stages VII and VIII.) In this respect contraction resembles expansion. The first stage of each brings the sharpest changes in quantity.[7] The maximum rates of decline in quantities are, in general, fairly close to the maximum rates of advance. Raw materials rise somewhat more sharply than they fall; manufactured goods, crop products, and nonmetallic minerals fall more sharply than they rise. But for most groups the differences are small, for quantities; the excess of rates of decline in buyers'

---

[5] Periods of maximum rate of decline in price and quantity, for the several commodity groups, are given below.

	INTERSTAGE PERIOD	AV. MONTHLY FALL IN PRICE
Crop products, domestic	VI-VII	—2.6
Producer goods for human consumption	VI-VII	—2.0
Raw materials	VI-VII	—2.0
American farm products	VI-VII	—1.8
Producer goods, all	VI-VII	—1.8
Human consumption goods	VI-VII	—1.6
Nondurable goods	VI-VII	—1.6
All commodities	*VI-VII*	*—1.5*
Capital equipment	VI-VII	—1.5
Metals	VI-VII	—1.5
Durable goods	VI-VII	—1.4
Foods	VI-VII	—1.4
Animal products, domestic	VI-VII & VII-VIII	—1.3
Other than American farm products	VII-VIII	—1.4
Consumer goods	VII-VIII	—1.3
Manufactured goods	VII-VIII	—1.3
Nonmetallic minerals	VII-VIII	—1.3

	INTERSTAGE PERIOD	AV. MONTHLY FALL IN QUANTITY
Metals	V-VI	—3.2
Capital equipment	V-VI	—3.0
Durable goods	V-VI & VII-VIII	—2.8
Other than American farm products	V-VI	—2.4
Manufactured goods	V-VI	—2.2
Producer goods, all	V-VI	—2.0
All commodities	*V-VI*	*—1.7*
Crop products, domestic	V-VI	—1.3
Producer goods for human consumption	V-VI	—1.3
Human consumption goods	V-VI	—1.2
Nondurable goods	V-VI	—1.2
Raw materials	V-VI & VI-VII	—1.2
Consumer goods	V-VI	—1.1
American farm products	V-VI	—1.0
Animal products, domestic	V-VI	—0.9
Foods	V-VI	—0.6
Nonmetallic minerals	VII-VIII	—2.3

[6] For raw materials and durable goods this rate is equaled in a later stage.

[7] As noted earlier, general indexes of industrial production, wider in coverage than our sample, are marked by rates of decline that increase from interstage period V-VI to period VI-VII.

outlays over the corresponding rates of advance during business expansion is largely attributable to differences in the behavior of the price factor.

In respect of prices, two points stand out. Without a single exception the maximum rates of price decline exceed the maximum rates of price advance during expansion.[8] The forces of price contraction seem to encounter fewer resistances than do the forces making for price rises in periods of general business expansion. The restraints on price increases—increases in supplies, governmental regulation, established and accepted price levels, the fear of inviting competition—appear to be stronger than the restraints on price decline, once general contraction is under way. Declines can build up to a higher tempo of price change.

The other point is a counterpart of this. Most commodity groups (about three-quarters of the total) attain their maximum rates of price decline between stages VI and VII of reference cycles. The remaining quarter have maximum rates of decline between stages VII and VIII. All groups, that is, are marked by rates of price decline that accelerate as contraction proceeds. No group attains its maximum in the initial period of business recession. In the expansion phase, it will be recalled, maximum rates of advance came for most groups in the first period of recovery, between reference cycle stages I and II. (Nonfarm products and, notably, products of heavy industry, were exceptions, having fairly constant rates of price advance until the final period of expansion when maximum rates were attained.) With the exceptions noted, retardation in the rate of price change after the initial rise is characteristic of business expansion; acceleration of price decline, at least through the second period of contraction and for some groups through the third interstage period, is characteristic of business contraction.[9]

---

[8] The fact that the net trend of prices was declining during the period covered has a clear bearing on this finding. More evidence, from other periods, is needed to confirm this indication.

[9] General indexes of wholesale prices show the same acceleration of decline, from the first to the second period of business contraction, with retardation thereafter. On expansions, maximum rates of price increase come in the first and

Extent of Outlay Changes

We have noted that 67 percent of the interstage movements of buyers' outlays were with the tide of cyclical change in the economy at large; 33 percent went counter to the general tide. With these figures in mind we examine the records of value changes for major commodity groups (Table 26).

Monetary payments for all classes of goods follow the tides of general business,[10] but there is considerable variation from group to group. The groups previously noted as having wide amplitudes of cyclical fluctuation—minerals, durable goods, capital equipment, nonfarm products—stand high in the present list. Roughly three-quarters of all interstage changes in buyers' outlays for these goods accord with the cyclical movements of general business; one-quarter reverse the cyclical tides. At the other extreme are farm products, nondurable goods, foods, and consumption goods generally. For these some 58 to 65 percent run with cyclical tides, 35 to 42 percent run counter to them. Products of domestic farm crops, the least disciplined of economic goods, the least subservient to strictly business influences, are at the bottom of the list, but even for these almost three-fifths of all value changes accord with the swings of busi-

---

fourth periods of expansion for one index, in the first period for one index, and in the first and second periods for one index. For none is the initial rise in price exceeded, although it may be equaled in later periods.

Interstage rates of change for the Bureau of Labor Statistics all commodities index covering 11 reference cycles between 1891 and 1938 (the 'war cycles' 1914-19 and 1919-21 are excluded), for the combined Warren-Pearson index and the BLS index covering 18 reference cycles (excluding war cycles) between 1854 and 1938, and for the Bradstreet index covering 9 reference cycles (excluding war cycles) between 1894 and 1933, are given below.

| | AV. MONTHLY RATES OF CHANGE IN WHOLESALE PRICE INDEXES | | |
INTERSTAGE PERIOD	BLS	Warren-Pearson and BLS	Bradstreet
I-II	+0.4	+0.4	+0.4
II-III	+0.2	+0.04	+0.4
III-IV	+0.3	+0.2	+0.2
IV-V	+0.4	+0.3	+0.2
V-VI	—0.1	—0.2	—0.4
VI-VII	—0.6	—0.8	—0.5
VII-VIII	—0.5	—0.4	—0.3
VIII-IX	—0.2	—0.4	+0.02

[10] In some degree the concordance of movement among groups is to be attributed to overlapping coverage.

TABLE 26

Interstage Movements of Buyers' Outlays for Groups of Commodities: Full Cycle

	NO. OF INTERSTAGE CHANGES	PERCENTAGE OF MOVEMENTS	
		With Cyclical Tide	Against Cyclical Tide
Metals	1,096	76	24
Durable goods	1,240	75	25
Capital equipment	1,384	74	26
Nonmetallic minerals	552	73	27
Other than American farm products	2,064	73	27
Producer goods, all	3,296	70	30
Manufactured goods	1,616	67	33
Producer goods for human consumption	2,096	67	33
All commodities	*4,160*	*67*	*33*
Raw materials	2,544	67	33
Human consumption goods	3,176	65	35
Animal products, domestic	1,360	63	37
Nondurable goods	2,856	63	37
American farm products	2,096	61	39
Consumer goods	1,232	61	39
Foods	1,720	60	40
Crop products, domestic	736	58	42

ness cycles. In their influence on monetary payments the forces of general business cycles are pervasive and compelling; after all allowance for the influence of overlapping categories, the degree of concordance with business tides among diverse classes of goods is impressive.[11]

The degree of conformity of outlay changes to the cyclical tide is higher during expansion (70 percent of all movements are with the tide) than during contraction (64 percent with the tide). This is true, also, for each commodity group studied. The manifestations of contraction are less pervasive than those of expansion,[12] a condition doubtless due in some degree to the upward push of secular forces in the American economy. Furthermore, the range of group differences, in percentage of outlay movements conforming to the cyclical tide, is greater in expansion than in contraction. The forces of business contraction appear to be more even in their incidence than those of expansion; i.e., expansion is marked by greater diversity of business fortunes.

Positive Movements of Outlay and Revenue
by Stages of Business Cycles

In Chapter 4 we discussed the behavior of aggregate monetary payments for commodities during the various stages of business cycles. We must go below the surface of aggregate payments if we are to have a just conception of the manner in which buyers' outlays (and sellers' revenues) respond to the forces of cyclical expansion and contraction. In what order and at what rate do outlays for different kinds of goods pick up after a general business depression? What is the timing and character of their declines, in contraction? What are the roles of price and quantity changes in the generation of expansions and contractions in outlays for different classes of goods?

---

[11] If we concentrate attention on average outlay patterns for individual commodities, subordinating aberrant movements occurring in particular business cycles, we may expect conformity to the general tides of business to be still higher. The following summary is based on a count of movements in these typical patterns.

	NO. OF INTERSTAGE CHANGES	PERCENTAGE OF MOVEMENTS	
		With Cyclical Tide	Against Cyclical Tide
Metals	120	95	5
Durable goods	152	92	8
Capital equipment	168	89	11
Other than American farm products	248	87	13
Producer goods, all	384	84	16
Nonmetallic minerals	80	82	18
Producer goods for human consumption	232	81	19
Raw materials	256	78	22
All commodities	512	77	23
Manufactured goods	256	76	24
Human consumption goods	392	73	27
Nondurable goods	352	70	30
Animal products, domestic	168	69	31
American farm products	264	67	33
Crop products, domestic	96	64	36
Foods	192	64	36
Consumer goods	176	63	37

When the details of individual cycles are thus ironed out the percentage of movement of outlays conforming to the cyclical tide is definitely higher, particularly in the heavy goods, nonfarm sectors. This is distinctly less true of the consumer goods, foods, and farm products sectors.

[12] This statement is based on observations taking account of *direction* of movement of buyers' outlays. In many cases there is retardation of advance during business contractions without absolute declines in monetary payments.

The business tide never runs unbrokenly in one direction. When contraction is most extensive, between reference cycle stages VI and VIII, about one-sixth of all commodities in our sample show increases in monetary values, in their average patterns. We may start the review of outlays for various classes of commodities with interstage period VII-VIII. Relevant observations are recorded in Table 27, col. 1 and 2. At the bottom of these columns are the products of heavy industries—producer goods, durable goods, nonfarm products, and goods for capital equipment. Declines in buyers' outlays and in sellers' revenues occur for 90 to 100 percent of goods of these types between stages VII and VIII of reference cycles. For farm products (notably crop products), consumer goods, and nondurable goods generally declines are less prevalent. Buyers' outlays actually increase for 23 to 33 percent of such goods at this period of general contraction.

During the final period of business contraction (stages VIII-IX) 45 percent of all commodities in our sample show positive value changes. But in each of six categories—human consumption goods, consumer goods, nondurables, farm products, foods, and crop products—the percentage exceeds 50 (see Table 27, col. 3 and 4). Among crop products, indeed, the percentage showing outlay increases is 92. The products of heavy industries —the goods marked by few outlay increases in the preceding period—are still at the bottom of the list, but for all 16 classes of goods the percentages of gains are greater than in the preceding period. The rate of contraction is being definitely retarded throughout the business system, although the tide is still ebbing.

In these terminal stages of business depression farm products and consumer goods are most resistant to the force of contraction, and most resilient in contributing to a business upturn. For substantial percentages of these goods, buyers' outlays increase before the ebb of general business has ended. We find here suggestions of the pressure of two sets of forces that may play initiatory roles in business revivals. There is an indication that recovery may get an early fillip from propitious changes (in prices or quantities, or both) affecting the values of farm products, particularly crop products, and swelling the purchasing power of farmers. From another direction—the increased buying of goods by consumers at large—may come other forces contributing to check the decline in monetary payments and to start an upturn at the strategic terminal point of the productive-distributive process.[18]

The nature of the flow of monetary payments for different types of commodity groups between reference cycle stages I and II is indicated in Table 27, col. 5 and 6. Now the general business tide has turned and is running strongly in the direction of recovery. An outstanding difference between this and the tabulation for the preceding period is found in the far greater homogeneity of the movement between stages I and II. Here the percentages of positive movements of values fall between 100 and 64 as compared with a range from 92 to 13 for interstage period VIII-IX. Quite remarkable, too, is the shift in the standing of particular groups. Durable goods and metals, which stand at the bottom of the list for period VIII-IX, with the lowest participation in outlay gains, now lead, with perfect scores. And consumer goods, crop products, and foods, which contributed substantially to recovery between stages VIII and IX are lowest in percentage of outlay increases between stages I and II. True, these goods are still gaining in value (except for crop products, more strongly than in the preceding period), but the procession is now led by other commodities. Rising demand for consumer goods and increasing revenues of farmers may play important roles in checking contraction and initiating recovery, but the ball is carried by other groups once expansion has definitely begun.

During the next three interstage periods (i.e., from stage II to the peak at stage V), the goods for which outlays increase most rapidly during the first period of expansion remain in the forefront (see Table 27, col. 7-12). Here are durable goods, metals, nonmetallic minerals, capital equipment, nonfarm products. Very large proportions of the commodities in these categories are marked by expanding buyers' outlays during the whole pe-

[18] This discussion does not, of course, cover the whole range of processes involved in business cycles. I do not suggest that the forces here named are ultimate causes.

TABLE 27

Changes in Buyers' Outlays during Interstage Periods in Business Cycles, by Commodity Groups

PERCENTAGE OF COMMODITIES IN GROUP SHOWING INCREASES IN OUTLAY

Interstage Period VII-VIII (1)	(2)	Interstage Period VIII-IX (3)	(4)
Crop products, domestic	33	Crop products, domestic	92
Consumer goods	32	Foods	63
Foods	29	American farm products	61
American farm products	24	Consumer goods	59
Nondurable goods	23	Nondurable goods	56
Human consumption goods	20	Human consumption goods	51
Animal products, domestic	19*	Producer goods for human consumption	48
Manufactured goods	19	Manufactured goods	47
All commodities	*17*	*All commodities*	*45*
Raw materials	16*	Animal products, domestic	43
Producer goods for human consumption	14	Raw materials	43
Capital equipment	10	Producer goods, all	37
Non-American farm products	10*	Nonmetallic minerals	30
Nonmetallic minerals	10*	Non-American farm products	29
Producer goods, all	10*	Capital equipment	24
Durable goods	5*	Durable goods	21
Metals	0*	Metals	13

Interstage Period I-II (5)	(6)	Interstage Period II-III (7)	(8)
Durable goods	100	Durable goods	95
Metals	100	Metals	93
Capital equipment	95	Nonmetallic minerals	90
Non-American farm products	94	Non-American farm products	87
Producer goods, all	94	Capital equipment	86
Nonmetallic minerals	90	Producer goods, all	69
Producer goods for human consumption	89	Raw materials	66
Raw materials	88	*All commodities*	*64*
All commodities	*84*	Manufactured goods	62
Animal products, domestic	81	Human consumption goods	58
Manufactured goods	81	Producer goods for human consumption	58
Human consumption goods	80	Consumer goods	55
Nondurable goods	77	Foods	50
American farm products	75	Nondurable goods	50
Crop products, domestic	67	Animal products, domestic	43
Foods	67	American farm products	42
Consumer goods	64	Crop products, domestic	41

TABLE 27 *(concl.)*

PERCENTAGE OF COMMODITIES IN GROUP SHOWING INCREASES IN OUTLAY

Interstage Period III-IV		Interstage Period IV-V	
(9)	(10)	(11)	(12)
Durable goods	100	Capital equipment	90
Metals	100	Nonmetallic minerals	90
Nonmetallic minerals	100	Durable goods	89
Non-American farm products	97	Non-American farm products	88
Capital equipment	95	Producer goods for human consumption	88
Manufactured goods	94	Metals	87
Producer goods, all	92	Producer goods, all	86
All commodities	*89*	Raw materials	86
Producer goods for human consumption	89	*All commodities*	*80*
Foods	88	Human consumption goods	77
Human consumption goods	88	Nondurable goods	76
Consumer goods	86	Crop products, domestic	75
Raw materials	85	Manufactured goods	75
Crop products, domestic	84	American farm products	74
Nondurable goods	84	Animal products, domestic	74
American farm products	82	Foods	69
Animal products, domestic	80	Consumer goods	63

Interstage Period V-VI		Interstage Period VI-VII	
(13)	(14)	(15)	(16)
Foods	46	Nonmetallic minerals	30
Consumer goods	45	Consumer goods	25*
Animal products, domestic	43	Foods	23*
Nonmetallic minerals	40	Animal products, domestic	19*
American farm products	33	American farm products	17*
Nondurable goods	30	Manufactured goods	17*
Human consumption goods	26	Nondurable goods	17*
Manufactured goods	26	*All commodities*	*16**
All commodities	*23*	Durable goods	16
Raw materials	21	Human consumption goods	16*
Crop products, domestic	16	Non-American farm products	16
Non-American farm products	12	Raw materials	16*
Producer goods, all	12	Capital equipment	14
Producer goods for human consumption	11	Crop products, domestic	12*
Capital equipment	5*	Producer goods, all	10*
Durable goods	5*	Metals	7
Metals	0*	Producer goods for human consumption	7*

* Percentage of positive value changes at its minimum for the cycle.

riod of reference expansion. Increased expenditures characterize markets for other goods as well, but the flow of outlays
(and revenues) never becomes as uniformly positive for consumption goods, farm products, and nondurables as it does for
their counterparts among capital equipment, nonfarm products,
and durable goods.

The marked check to expansion after stage II that appears
in the record for aggregate outlays is manifest in the detailed
story. Among the 16 here listed only one group (nonmetallic
minerals) fails to reflect retardation. It is most evident in the
lower half of the list, among human consumption goods, nondurables, foods, and farm products. For farm products, indeed,
declines in outlay actually exceed increases between stages II
and III. (Only for this group, with its constituents, animal products and crop products, do outlay decreases exceed increases in
any period of general expansion between stages I and V.) That
this check to expansion after the first upsurge is greatest among
nondurables and among goods destined for human consumption is a suggestive fact.[14] We have already remarked upon the
early initiation of recovery among these goods. To this we now
add evidence indicative of some satiation of demand, or of lessened prospects for profitable sale, after a relatively brief revival. Perhaps the most striking feature of this evidence is the
fact that the degree of decline between interstage periods I-II
and II-III is materially higher for goods in the consumption,
nondurable categories than for products of heavy industry, although the latter are, in the full cycle, subject to fluctuations
over a much wider range. There are signs here of a distinctive
rhythm and timing in the buying of nondurable goods intended
for human consumption, a tempo and type of fluctuation somewhat different from those found among heavier products. These
clues to possible interrelations among cyclical processes call for
further study.

14 The percentage of consumer goods for which outlays are expanding shows a
drop of only 9 points between interstage periods I-II and II-III, while the
drop is 31 points for producer goods for human consumption. The latter group
includes goods intended for human consumption but not yet finally processed.
Actual consumption may be checked somewhat, but buying is most seriously
restricted at the producer goods stage for consumption goods.

Pervasive recovery is resumed after stage III (see Table 27, col. 9 and 10). Consumption goods, nondurables, foods, and farm products swing back 30 to 40 points on the percentage scale—movements of a magnitude far exceeding those for the generally more sensitive heavy goods.[15] The short 'cycle' that occurs midway in general business expansion seems to affect, predominantly, nondurable goods flowing from farms into the consumption sector of the economy.

One other aspect of the check to expansion after stage II and the resumption after stage III is noteworthy. The percentage of manufactured goods showing increases in buyers' outlays drops sharply after stage II (only 62 percent show increases between stages II and III, as compared with 81 percent between stages I and II), but recovers rapidly to the highest value for the cycle (94) between stages III and IV. This period is the only one during expansion when the percentage of outlay increases is greater for manufactured goods than for raw materials. Between stages III and IV, apparently, recovery is substantial and pervasive. The range of group differences, in respect of degree of participation in outlay expansion, is less than at any other period of the cycle.

The scope of outlay expansion shrinks between stages IV and V (Table 27, col. 11 and 12). After stage V the cyclical current is abruptly reversed (Table 27, col. 13 and 14). For all commodities the percentage of positive changes in buyers' outlays falls sharply from 80 between stages IV and V to 23 between stages V and VI. In other words, for 57 percent of all commodities increases in the total expenditures of buyers change to decreases. This is a substantially greater shift than the reverse movement after stage IX, which affects only 39 percent of all commodities (the 57 and 39 are both net figures).

In the movement of buyers' outlays between stages V and VI the roles of different categories of goods shift again, fundamentally. For less than one-quarter of all commodities (23 percent) outlays are still rising from stage V to stage VI, but the groups that rank high in this respect are in general those that

15 These percentages relate, of course, to proportions of commodities in given categories, not to degree of fluctuation.

trailed during expansion. Outlays are relatively well maintained for consumer goods, farm products, nondurables, while outlays for metals, durable goods, capital equipment, producer goods, nonfarm products, drop sharply. As in the shift after stage I the two ends of the spectrum are almost completely reversed after stage V. (Nonmetallic minerals are in the upper half of the rankings in the periods just before and just after the peak, and products of farm crops remain in the lower half. The positions of the other 14 groups are reversed.)

Between stages VI and VII the proportion of commodities for which outlays increase falls to 16 percent. Declines prevail in all classes (see Table 27, col. 15 and 16). Group differences are distinctly smaller than in the preceding period; cross-currents are fewer. In general, the groups for which positive changes were relatively frequent between stages V and VI lead the list between stages VI and VII. Notably above the general average are nonmetallic minerals and consumer goods. Outlay changes for producer goods, metals, and capital equipment are predominantly negative.

As we return to interstage period VII-VIII (see Table 27, col. 1 and 2) we complete the cycle. For the over-all group the scope of contraction is slightly less than in the preceding period; 83 percent of the outlay changes are negative, 17 percent positive. But cross-currents are present. Contraction persists for durables, nonfarm products, capital equipment, metals, and nonmetallic minerals. In each of these groups buyers' outlays are declining for more goods than in the preceding period. For consumer goods, farm products, nondurables, and human consumption goods generally, recovery is beginning. Gains in buyers' outlays are still outweighed by losses, but there are more positive changes than between stages VI and VII. Some of the seeds of the general expansion that still lies well ahead are beginning to sprout here.

We have traced, stage by stage of business cycles, the swellings and contractions of the stream of monetary payments that flows from buyers of commodities to sellers. We have noted the relative stability of outlays for goods in the consumer, nondurable, and farm product sectors of the economy, and the wider variations of outlays for producer goods and the products of heavy industries. With the greater stability of the former groups appears to go a definite leadership in the checking of contraction and in the initiation of recovery. Not only does the proportion of positive changes in outlays remain higher, for these groups, during contractions; such goods predominate among those for which outlays are increasing while contraction is still general in the economy. We may not say that these changes are ultimately causal in the complex processes of business cycles, but they are significant links in the network of sequences that lead from depression to recovery, and from prosperity to recession.

Behind all these changes in monetary outlays lie shifts in the number of physical units of goods traded, and changes in average unit price. What part does each of these factors play in the movements of outlays and revenues during business cycles? To this question we now turn, breaking into the cyclical process between stages VI and VIII of the general cycle.

Relative Roles of Price and Quantity Factors in Determining the Extent of Increases in Buyers' Outlays

For a varying proportion of commodities, as we have seen, outlays expand even in the worst months of contraction and depression; for a certain proportion, outlays contract, even in the most prosperous times. Changes in unit prices and in quantities contribute to these expansions and contractions of monetary payments, in degrees that vary from group to group of commodities. The story, in detail, is somewhat complex, but certain clear patterns emerge. In defining these we give chief attention to the roles of price and quantity factors in the shifts that occur from period to period in the proportion of commodities for which buyers' outlays and sellers' revenues increase. This concentration on increments and decrements helps to illuminate dynamic aspects of the problem. The basic observations for this review are set forth in Appendix Table 4. The entries in the ensuing text tables (28 to 35) are the first differences of the measures there given.

In exploring the relative changes of prices and quantities as contributors to cyclical expansions and contractions in the stream of monetary payments, we start with the first manifestations of recovery after stage VII. (The reference is, of course, to the range of phenomena here studied.) The proportion of positive changes in outlays for commodities at large is almost the same in interstage period VII-VIII as in period VI-VII, but significant differences are discernible in the detailed record, by groups. Table 28 shows for each of 16 commodity groups the change in the percentage of commodities gaining in value between periods VI-VII and VII-VIII, and indicates the part played by price and quantity components in each change. Eight groups, predominantly those from the consumer goods, farm products, nondurable goods sectors of the economy, show increases in the percentage of commodities marked by outlay advances between these two periods. We have already noted the

TABLE 28

Changes between Interstage Periods VI-VII and VII-VIII
in Percentages of Commodities for Which Buyers' Outlays Increase,
by Commodity Groups

| | CHANGE IN PERCENTAGE VI-VII TO VII-VIII | | |
| | | Prices | Quantities |
	Total	Dominant	Dominant
Crop products, domestic	+21	—2	+23
American farm products	+7	—1	+8
Consumer goods	+7	—8	+15
Producer goods for human consumption	+7	0	+7
Foods	+6	—3	+9
Nondurable goods	+6	—4	+10
Human consumption goods	+4	—4	+8
Manufactured goods	+2	—1	+3
All commodities	+*1*	—*3*	+*4*
Animal products, domestic	0	0	0
Producer goods, all	0	0	0
Raw materials	0	—5	+5
Capital equipment	—4	0	—4
Other than American farm products	—6	—5	—1
Metals	—7	0	—7
Durable goods	—11	0	—11
Nonmetallic minerals	—20	—10	—10

The base of each percentage is the number of commodities in the group in question.

positive role of goods of this type in supporting the forces of recovery while contraction is still general. The outstanding fact now to be emphasized is that in every case the increase in the percentage of commodities showing outlay advances is attributable to the quantity factor. For all groups the influence of prices is negative, or neutral, as a factor making for the extension of buyers' outlays.

As we pass stage VIII of reference cycles we come into a period in which, although the general drift of outlay changes is still a declining one, a large number of commodities—45 percent of the total—show increases in the amounts spent by buyers. (See Table 27. This represents an increase of 28 over the figure for interstage period VII-VIII.) In Table 29 we have a record of the percentages of commodities gaining in value, by groups, between interstage periods VII-VIII and VIII-IX. The impetus to expansion in buyers' outlays comes, predominantly, from those sectors in which signs of recovery were manifest in the preceding period, i.e., among foods, consumption goods,

TABLE 29

Changes between Interstage Periods VII-VIII and VIII-IX in Percentages of Commodities for Which Buyers' Outlays Increase, by Commodity Groups

| | | CHANGE IN PERCENTAGE VII-VIII TO VIII-IX | |
	Total	Prices Dominant	Quantities Dominant
Crop products, domestic	+59	+29	+30
American farm products	+37	+17	+20
Foods	+34	+13	+21
Producer goods for human consumption	+34	+12	+22
Nondurable goods	+33	+12	+21
Human consumption goods	+31	+11	+20
Manufactured goods	+28	+9	+19
All commodities	+28	+9	+19
Consumer goods	+27	+9	+18
Producer goods, all	+27	+8	+19
Raw materials	+27	+9	+18
Animal products, domestic	+24	+10	+14
Nonmetallic minerals	+20	+5	+15
Other than American farm products	+19	+2	+17
Durable goods	+16	+3	+13
Capital equipment	+14	+2	+12
Metals	+13	0	+13

farm products, and nondurable goods generally. In the reenforcing of recovery among these goods, and the general reversal of movement discernible in the outlay changes among other categories of goods, price and quantity factors supplement each other. It is noteworthy that there are no negative entries in Table 29. The current of contraction is still ebbing, but all changes are positive. Although prices supplement quantities in working to reverse the prevalent decline in monetary payments, the quantity factor is dominant in all the groups listed.

As we round the turn at stage IX we pass the low point of business cycles in the economy at large. Of our full list of commodities, 84 percent show positive value changes between stages I and II, an increase of 39 percent over interstage period VIII-IX. The changes occurring in the transition from the final period of contraction to the initial period of general recovery are set forth in Table 30. We have noted that, typically, products of the heavy industries move to the fore at this stage of recovery. Such industries, together with nonfarm products

TABLE 30

Changes between Interstage Periods VIII-IX and I-II
in Percentages of Commodities for Which Buyers' Outlays Increase,
by Commodity Groups

| | | CHANGE IN PERCENTAGE VIII-IX TO I-II | |
	Total	Prices Dominant	Quantities Dominant
Metals	+87	+13	+74
Durable goods	+79	+13	+66
Capital equipment	+71	+17	+54
Other than American farm products	+65	+24	+41
Nonmetallic minerals	+60	+25	+35
Producer goods, all	+57	+30	+27
Raw materials	+45	+32	+13
Producer goods for human consumption	+41	+36	+5
All commodities	*+39*	*+25*	*+14*
Animal products, domestic	+38	+28	+10
Manufactured goods	+34	+19	+15
Human consumption goods	+29	+30	−1
Nondurable goods	+21	+31	−10
American farm products	+14	+25	−11
Consumer goods	+5	+23	−18
Foods	+4	+29	−25
Crop products, domestic	−25	+21	−46

and producer goods, are marked by shifts in the direction of positive value changes affecting more than 50 percent of their component commodities. The changes after stage IX are marked, too, by a revealing contrast in the roles of prices and quantities. The classes of goods in the lower half of Table 30—commodities chiefly drawn from the foods, consumer goods, nondurable goods, and farm products sectors of the economy—show increases in the percentages of commodities gaining in value predominantly because of price advances. Among the classes of commodities in the upper half of Table 30, quantity increases are the chief factor in the advances in the percentages of commodities gaining in value. The sole exceptions are raw materials, producer goods, and producer goods destined for human consumption. The third category, indeed, is marked by a notable increase in prices.

This evidence points to the presence, at a very early stage of recovery, of pressure on the supplies of certain classes of goods —notably farm products and goods intended for, or ready for, human consumption. These classes of goods, as we have observed, cannot readily be increased in volume on short notice. Prices, accordingly, reflect the pressure of new demand early in general business expansion. For the heavier goods, primarily nonfarm products, increases in demand have been more recently generated and, at the same time, supply is in general more expansible on short notice. Consequently, price pressures are less pronounced for such goods. Buyers' outlays increase, primarily, because more goods are changing hands.

We have noted the characteristic check to the scope of expansion that comes after stage II of reference cycles. The general economy is still expanding, but retarding influences manifest themselves in many sectors. This check is illuminatingly revealed by the changes recorded in Table 31. Not one group of commodities listed in Table 31 shows an increase in the percentage of goods gaining in value at this stage of reference cycles. Nonmetallic minerals hold constant; all other groups are marked by declines, affecting from 5 to 38 percent of the commodities in the several classes. For crop products alone does the quantity factor exert a positive influence in the changes

TABLE 31

Changes between Interstage Periods I-II and II-III
in Percentages of Commodities for Which Buyers' Outlays Increase,
by Commodity Groups

| | | CHANGE IN PERCENTAGE I-II TO II-III | |
| | | Prices | Quantities |
	Total	Dominant	Dominant
Nonmetallic minerals	0	+20	—20
Durable goods	—5	+3	—8
Metals	—7	+4	—11
Other than American farm products	—7	+1	—8
Capital equipment	—9	—2	—7
Consumer goods	—9	—9	0
Foods	—17	—13	—4
Manufactured goods	—19	—5	—14
All commodities	—20	—7	—13
Human consumption goods	—22	—12	—10
Raw materials	—22	—10	—12
Producer goods, all	—25	—8	—17
Crop products, domestic	—26	—42	+16
Nondurable goods	—27	—13	—14
Producer goods for human consumption	—31	—17	—14
American farm products	—33	—15	—18
Animal products, domestic	—38	0	—38

here recorded. For all except 5 of the 16 groups the quantity factor dominates the price factor in a negative direction. Prices are more important, negatively, than quantities among foods, consumer goods, consumption goods, and crop products. For certain minerals and durable goods prices make for advancing outlays at this stage. But, in general, the forces of retardation are apparent in a reduction of the percentage of commodities marked by rising prices as well as in a decline in the percentage for which physical volume is increasing.

After stage III there is another considerable increase in the percentage of commodities marked by expanding buyers' outlays. Between stages III and IV, indeed, comes the most compact and uniform expansion of buyers' outlays and revenues of sellers (see Table 27, col. 9 and 10). The parts played by prices and quantities in this upward surge are shown in Table 32. We have remarked above that it is the normally stable consumption segment of the economy that is, at this stage, characterized by the sharpest swing back toward recovery. These goods

TABLE 32

Changes between Interstage Periods II-III and III-IV
in Percentages of Commodities for Which Buyers' Outlays Increase,
by Commodity Groups

| | | CHANGE IN PERCENTAGE II-III TO III-IV | |
	Total	Prices Dominant	Quantities Dominant
Crop products, domestic	+43	+38	+5
American farm products	+40	+8	+32
Foods	+38	+11	+27
Animal products, domestic	+37	—10	+47
Nondurable goods	+34	+7	+27
Manufactured goods	+32	+8	+24
Consumer goods	+31	+11	+20
Producer goods for human consumption	+31	+10	+21
Human consumption goods	+30	+9	+21
All commodities	+25	+10	+15
Producer goods, all	+23	+9	+14
Raw materials	+19	+13	+6
Nonmetallic minerals	+10	—5	+15
Other than American farm products	+10	+13	—3
Capital equipment	+9	+19	—10
Metals	+7	+23	—16
Durable goods	+5	+20	—15

participate in the general expansion between stages I and V somewhat less completely than do goods drawn from the heavy industry sector, but in the intensity of the resumption of advance after the check between stages II and III farm products, nondurables, and consumption goods generally lead the way. This resumption of expansion reflects increases in both prices and quantities. It is to be noted, however, that at this stage of expansion quantity increases are dominant in the consumption goods and nondurable sectors, while price increases are relatively more important among durable goods, metals, capital equipment, and nonfarm products generally. Indeed, for each of these last four categories the percentage of commodities gaining in value by reason of quantity changes actually decreases as we pass from period II-III to period III-IV. It appears that limitations to volume expansion, previously felt in the consumer, nondurable goods sector of the economy, are experienced after stage III among heavier goods.

The interplay of factors of supply and demand is traced further in Table 33, dealing with the final period of general expansion. A positive tide is still running strongly; 80 percent of all commodities show increases in buyers' outlays between

TABLE 33

Changes between Interstage Periods III-IV and IV-V
in Percentages of Commodities for Which Buyers' Outlays Increase,
by Commodity Groups

| | | CHANGE IN PERCENTAGE III-IV TO IV-V | |
	Total	Prices Dominant	Quantities Dominant
Raw materials	+1	—8	+9
Producer goods for human consumption	—1	+2	—3
Capital equipment	—5	—17	+12
Animal products, domestic	—6	+8	—14
Producer goods, all	—6	—5	—1
American farm products	—8	+3	—11
Nondurable goods	—8	0	—8
Crop products, domestic	—9	—4	—5
All commodities	—9	—5	—4
Other than American farm products	—9	—14	+5
Nonmetallic minerals	—10	—25	+15
Durable goods	—11	—18	+7
Human consumption goods	—11	—2	—9
Metals	—13	—20	+7
Foods	—19	+4	—23
Manufactured goods	—19	—3	—16
Consumer goods	—23	—7	—16

stages IV and V (Table 27). This, however, is a decline of 9 from the percentage (89) for interstage period III-IV. In period IV-V all commodity groups except raw materials show drops in the percentages of commodities gaining in value. Responsibility for these declines is about evenly divided between prices and quantities. For capital equipment, nonfarm products, nonmetallic minerals, durable goods, and metals, prices are the dominant factor in checking increases in outlays. It will be recalled that these are the classes of goods for which prices were the primary factor in the outlay increases shown in Table 32. With retardation after stage IV prices play less of a boosting role in the markets for these goods. On the other side we have farm products, nondurables, consumption goods generally, and manufactured goods. For these, quantities are the dominant factor in reducing the scope of outlay increases. The shifting pendulum checks quantity advances in this sector after the rather extensive increases of period III-IV.

With the passing of the peak at stage V the sharpest decline of the whole cycle occurs in the proportion of commodities for which buyers' outlays are advancing. For 57 percent of commodities, gains in aggregate monetary value change to losses. The greatest drops, for which quantity is predominantly responsible, occur among metals, capital equipment, durables, and producer goods generally (Table 34). For three groups only—animal products, foods, and producer goods destined for human consumption—is price a more powerful depressant than quantity. The foods group alone is marked by pronounced price predominance.

TABLE 34

Changes between Interstage Periods IV-V and V-VI
in Percentages of Commodities for Which Buyers' Outlays Increase,
by Commodity Groups

| | CHANGE IN PERCENTAGE IV-V TO V-VI | | |
	Total	Prices Dominant	Quantities Dominant
Consumer goods	—18	0	—18
Foods	—23	—19	—4
Animal products, domestic	—31	—17	—14
American farm products	—41	—20	—21
Nondurable goods	—46	—21	—25
Manufactured goods	—49	—15	—34
Nonmetallic minerals	—50	0	—50
Human consumption goods	—51	—22	—29
All commodities	—57	—20	—37
Crop products, domestic	—59	—26	—33
Raw materials	—65	—24	—41
Producer goods, all	—74	—30	—44
Other than American farm products	—76	—20	—56
Producer goods for human consumption	—77	—39	—38
Durable goods	—84	—21	—63
Capital equipment	—85	—19	—66
Metals	—87	—20	—67

In the second period of general business contraction (between stages VI and VII) the proportion of commodities gaining in value shrinks still further (see Table 35); fewer commodities are affected, however. The categories in which outlay increases

are at a minimum are still chiefly the heavy durables and producer goods (see Table 27), but the shifts of position, from
outlay gains to losses, are most numerous among the lighter
consumer goods that lagged in the preceding stage of contrac-

TABLE 35

Changes between Interstage Periods V-VI and VI-VII
in Percentages of Commodities for Which Buyers' Outlays Increase,
by Commodity Groups

| | CHANGE IN PERCENTAGE V-VI TO VI-VII | | |
| | | Prices | Quantities |
	Total	Dominant	Dominant
Durable goods	+11	0	+11
Capital equipment	+9	0	+9
Metals	+7	0	+7
Other than American farm products	+4	−1	+5
Producer goods, all	−2	−4	+2
Crop products, domestic	−4	−14	+10
Producer goods for human consumption	−4	−4	0
Raw materials	−5	−7	+2
All commodities	−7	−9	+2
Manufactured goods	−9	−12	+3
Human consumption goods	−10	−10	0
Nonmetallic minerals	−10	−10	0
Nondurable goods	−13	−12	−1
American farm products	−16	−17	+1
Consumer goods	−20	−19	−1
Foods	−23	−22	−1
Animal products, domestic	−24	−19	−5

tion. Price declines are now dominant in the direction of contraction. In no case is the influence of price positive. For four
groups increases in quantities changing hands are strong enough
to bring actual increases in the proportion of goods marked by
gains in outlays. At this stage of contraction price is the primary
factor tending to change outlay gains to losses. This negative
role of the price factor extends into the next period, while
physical quantities continue to exert some positive pressures.
But this has been dealt with on an earlier page (Table 28). The
circle has been completed.

⟨ CHAPTER 6 ⟩

SUMMARY

IN this study we are investigating the interactions of commodity prices and physical quantities during cycles in general business, and cyclical fluctuations in the monetary outlays of buyers (and the revenues of sellers) of commodities. Our first concern is with the mechanism by which demand and supply of individual commodities are kept in some kind of equilibrium as the business system passes through alternating phases of cyclical expansion and contraction. We are seeking to define patterns of behavior characteristic of the markets for individual commodities and for major classes of commodities as these markets react to the pressures of cyclical change. Secondly, we are concerned with the flows and ebbs of monetary payments for commodities, individually and in the aggregate, during cycles in general business. Changes in the monetary stream reflect variations in the number of physical units exchanged and shifts in unit prices, but these two factors differ greatly in relative importance from area to area of economic activity. We are interested, therefore, not only in the patterns of variation in monetary payments in various markets, but also in the relative roles of price and physical volume as factors in cyclical changes in buyers' outlays and sellers' revenues.

Interactions of Unit Prices and Quantities in Business Cycles

1) About five-sixths of all the commodities studied are marked by persistent and significant patterns of behavior, in the combined movements of prices and quantities during cycles in general business.

2) There is extraordinary diversity among commodities in the magnitude of the variation of prices and quantities. The combined variability of prices and quantities for coke, at one extreme, is 69 times that of flour, at the other.

3) There is equally wide diversity in the relative importance of the price and quantity components. The price contribution to the combined variability ranges from 1 percent of the total,

for iron ore and passenger automobiles, to 98 percent, for crude petroleum and potatoes.

4) Prices participate in business cycles more extensively than quantities, when the criterion is direction of movement. This is true of both expansion and contraction, but more notably of contraction. Physical volume reverses the cyclical push more frequently than price. This contracyclical movement of quantity series is strongest during business contractions, when secular pressures often more than offset cyclical influences.

5) In magnitude of relative movement, the net effect of business expansion is to raise quantities more than prices; the net effect of business contraction is to reduce prices more than quantities. (Trend factors in both volume and price play parts here, of course. We are dealing with the combined effects of cyclical movements and intracycle trends.) Various measures of the degree to which these two factors respond to cyclical forces indicate that quantities are more sensitive to pressures of expansion, prices to those of contraction. The brakes to expansion seem to be stronger for prices than for quantities; the brakes to contraction seem to be stronger for quantities than for prices. (These are over-all statements, concerning the aggregate of all commodities here studied. Groups vary widely in this respect.)

6) Measures of the full cycle elasticity of quantities and the flexibility of unit prices (for explanation of the technical meanings of these terms see Ch. 2) are positive for 44 of the 64 commodities studied. In other words, inverse relations between quantities and unit prices characterize only about 30 percent of these commodities when market behavior is studied in the framework of reference cycles. For most commodities the cyclical pressures making for concurrent increases in prices and quantities, and for concurrent declines, override such market tendencies as may make for inverse movements of prices and quantities. In the price-quantity relations of business cycles the patterns of static theory are subordinated to dynamic forces that bring changes in the position and shape of demand and supply curves. Diversity in the relative responsiveness of quantities and prices to cyclical forces is revealed by measures of

106

price flexibility (full cycle) ranging from values very close to zero for passenger automobiles and iron ore, to $+50$ for meat and -50 for potatoes.

7) In the average pattern of cyclical behavior, for all 64 commodities, physical quantities show a slight advance in the terminal period of general business contraction (between stages VIII and IX) when prices are still sagging. The average rate of advance in quantities exceeds that in prices for all periods up to the reference peak at stage V, except during the characteristic retardation that occurs between stages II and III. In contraction the initial fall in quantities (between stages V and VI) is more rapid than in prices. In all subsequent stages of contraction prices decline more sharply.

8) This same average pattern, for all commodities, yields coefficients of quantity elasticity and price flexibility for the full cycle that differ but slightly ($e=+1.01$; $f=+0.99$). Notable, however, are the markedly lower elasticity of quantities and the markedly higher flexibility of prices in the contraction phase of reference cycles, as compared with measures for expansion. Measures for the separate interstage periods reveal progressive increases in the sensitivity of quantities as general business expansion spreads after reference cycle stage III. (Retardation between stages II and III is marked by a sharp drop in the elasticity of quantities, a sharp advance in the flexibility of prices.) In the middle and terminal phases of contraction we find, conversely, progressive increases in the flexibility of unit prices.

9) Commodity groups differ greatly in the combined cyclical variability of prices and quantities. The average joint variability of metals is seven times that of consumer goods. In general, durable goods, capital equipment, and nonfarm products show high joint variability, while consumer goods, foods, farm products, and nondurables show low variability.

10) Among commodity groups the contribution of the price factor to the combined variability of prices and quantities ranges from 16 percent for durable goods to 96 percent for crop products. Price variability is high, relative to variability of quantities, in markets close to the initial stage of extraction

and in markets close to the final stage of consumption. Relative stability of output of many primary products (for which supply cannot be altered on short notice on the basis of market prospects) places the chief burden of cyclical adaptation on prices. Relative stability of consumption, especially of nondurable goods, plays a similar role at the terminal stage of the distributive process. In the intermediate markets, especially those for durable goods, capital equipment, and nonfarm products, prices are more stable, and quantity variations reflect mainly the play of cyclical forces.

11) An outstanding characteristic of the 16 commodity groups we have studied is their relative homogeneity in the magnitude of their price variability (crop products, at one extreme, are slightly more than twice as variable as consumer goods, at the other); their extraordinary heterogeneity in variability of physical quantities (the measure for metals, the most variable, is 144 times that for foods, the most stable). This difference is the more notable in that the price and quantity averages for all commodities are fairly close, the price average being slightly higher. Ties among the elements of the price system, making for uniformity of response to cyclical forces, are far closer than those among physical quantities.

12) Group measures of quantity elasticity and price flexibility during the full cycle cover a wide range. For durable goods the flexibility of prices is measured by a coefficient of .43; for foods the coefficient is 50. All measures are positive. The grouping process gives predominance to the cyclical forces that make for concurrent advances, or concurrent declines, in prices and quantities. Flexible prices (and inelastic quantities) are found among farm products, nondurable goods, consumption goods of all sorts, and raw materials; inflexible prices (and elastic quantities) characterize their counterparts—nonfarm products, durable goods, capital goods, and manufactured goods. We find among the separate groups, as we did for the aggregate of all commodities, a characteristic decline in quantity elasticity (and an increase in price flexibility) as expansion gives way to contraction.

Patterns of Buyers' Outlays and Sellers' Revenues
in Business Cycles: Aggregative

13) The amplitudes of fluctuations in quantities and in average unit prices, in reference cycles, are about equal (amplitude indexes of 40). The corresponding cyclical swings in buyers' outlays are twice as great (amplitude index of 80). These relations result from the fact that cyclical variation in unit prices and in quantities reenforce each other, being roughly concurrent and in the same direction. The impress of business cycles upon the stream of monetary payments is thus accentuated.

14) The rate of increase in buyers' outlays is highest during the first period of general expansion (between reference cycle stages I and II). A definite check is experienced after stage II, followed by a steady advance that continues to the peak of general business at stage V. A sharp reversal of movement comes at stage V, the decline is accelerated after stage VI, and slightly retarded after stage VII. In the final period of contraction there is virtual stagnation of buyers' outlays for one whole interstage period, in contrast to the immediate reversal that comes as the peak of expansion is passed.

15) Monetary payments, viewed in detail and at all stages of business cycles, move in general with the tide of business at large. Of the aggregate of interstage changes in payments for individual commodities, just two-thirds are with the cyclical tide, one-third against (the proportion of movements with the tide is slightly higher than this in expansion, slightly lower in contraction). The nature of business cycles, as preponderant tendencies toward expansion or contraction, rather than completely uniform advances or declines, is manifest in this overall record.

16) At any stage of a business cycle monetary payments will be increasing for some commodities, decreasing for others. The proportion of transactions involving increases in buyers' outlays is at a minimum between reference cycle stages VI and VIII, when outlays were increasing for about one-sixth of all commodities studied. (The reference is to the average behavior of individual commodities.) Outlays were declining for the

other five-sixths. Between stages VIII and IX the tide is still receding, but the ebb runs far less strongly. Buyers are increasing their outlays for 45 percent of all commodities. During reference expansion, between stages I and V, outlays are increasing for 80 percent or more of all commodities, except during the brief period of retardation after stage II. Between stages III and IV, when 89 percent of all outlay changes are positive, the stream of monetary payments is running more uniformly in one direction than it is at any other period of the cycle. The reversal after stage V brings a sharper shift than did the counter-reversal at the cyclical trough. Here, in respect of the scope of the cyclical movement, the story is the same as for the rate of movement. Transition from expansion to contraction is a sharp, quick change; that from contraction to expansion is slower, and more protracted.

17) Quantity changes are chiefly responsible for the cyclical expansions and contractions in monetary payments between buyers and sellers of commodities. In 58 percent of more than four thousand interstage changes in buyers' outlays quantity is the dominant factor in determining the direction and amount of the observed movement of monetary values. Price was dominant in the other 42 percent.

18) In each of the four periods between stages I and V of reference expansions increases in physical quantity are the dominant factor in about 60 percent of all outlay increases. Only between stages V and VI, after the peak of business expansion, does price become more important than quantity as a boosting factor among the small minority of goods for which outlays are still increasing. The dominance of quantity in making for increases in monetary payments is high in the final period of general business contraction when it works to reverse the prevalent decline in buyers' outlays and sellers' revenues.

19) As a factor depressing monetary outlays quantity is strongest, relatively, when the cyclical tide is turning between stages IV and VI, and in the check to expansion between stages II and III. This temporary retardation seems to be primarily a physical phenomenon. Price as a depressant is strongest in the middle period of contraction, between stages VI and VIII.

20) In summary of the aggregative record, the evidence examined indicates that the force of expanding volume in the physical quantity of goods produced and exchanged is dominant in braking the decline in buyers' outlays and sellers' revenues in the final stages of business contraction; that quantity declines interrupt the general advance after stage II and play a leading role in the generation of recession; that prices follow the leader in expansion, turn downward with quantities after the peak of business activity has been passed (but work in an appreciable minority of cases to keep monetary payments rising during the first stage of general business contraction), and push strongly to reenforce contraction in the stream of monetary payments.

Patterns of Buyers' Outlays and Sellers' Revenues in Business Cycles: Commodity Groups

21) The 16 commodity groups here studied are alike in that buyers' outlays reach a maximum at stage V of reference cycles, and decline thereafter. At reference cycle troughs there is greater divergence. For 5 groups (farm products, crop products, consumer goods, foods, and nondurable goods) buyers' outlays begin to expand after stage VIII. For 3 groups (raw materials, animal products, and goods intended for human consumption) outlays are constant between stages VIII and IX. For the other 8 groups they reach a minimum at stage IX.

22) Differences among groups in amplitude of outlay fluctuations are much greater than are differences in timing. Fluctuations of buyers' outlays in business cycles are narrowest for foods, consumer goods, farm products, and nondurables; they are widest for metals, durables, and goods for capital equipment. In general, group differences in amplitude of outlay fluctuations are closely correlated with group differences in amplitude of cyclical swings in physical volume. The relative uniformity of price changes previously noted is characteristic of these commodity groups. Differences in the susceptibility of quantities to cyclical forces are the chief factors making for differences in the cyclical amplitudes of buyers' outlays.

23) Buyers' outlays for foods increase most rapidly in the

terminal period of general business contraction (between stages VIII and IX of reference cycles). For nearly all other groups (13 of the 16) rates of advancing outlays are highest in the first period of reference expansion (between stages I and II). For the broad class of consumer goods the maximum rate of advance comes midway in the general period of expansion (between stages III and IV). Foods and consumer goods generally attain maximum rates of increase in physical quantities in the final period of reference contraction (between stages VIII and IX). This early physical recovery in the consumer sector of the economy is a significant aspect of the transition from contraction to expansion in the economy at large.

24) The sharpest accelerations in outlays are chiefly attributable to increases in the physical volume of purchases. For four groups only (farm products, crop products, producer goods for human consumption, and nondurables), goods for which supply does not respond promptly to the stimulus of new demand, were price increases the chief factors in these maximum rates.

25) For all groups except animal products and foods maximum rates of decline in buyers' outlays are greater than maximum rates of advance.

26) Maximum rates of decline in buyers' outlays come for most commodity groups in the second period of general business contraction (between stages VI and VII). There is, thus, acceleration of decline from the first to the second period of recession, in contrast to the characteristic retardation of advance during expansion. Exceptions to the early acceleration in contraction are found among manufactured goods, crop products, and farm products generally, for which outlay declines are most intense in the first period of business decline. For consumer goods acceleration continues to a maximum decline in buyers' outlays between reference cycle stages VII and VIII.

27) The maximum rates of decline in quantities differ but slightly from maximum rates of advance for most commodity groups. Rates of price decline that exceed rates of price advance are largely responsible for rates of decline in buyers' outlays that exceed corresponding rates of advance. These price de-

clines, we have noted, are marked by acceleration at least through the second period of contraction, and for some groups through the third period—acceleration that stands in notable contrast to the retardation characteristic of price advances during business expansions.

28) Buyers' outlays for all classes of goods follow the tides of expansion and contraction in business at large, but the extent of concordance varies somewhat from group to group. For metals, durable goods, capital equipment, and nonagricultural products about three-quarters of all interstage movements of buyers' outlays accord with the cyclical movements of general business. The proportion falls to about three-fifths for the groups of goods least subservient to the forces of business cycles —consumer goods, farm products, and nondurable goods. The range of difference is not wide. The impressive feature is that from 60 to 75 percent of the interstage movements of monetary payments for goods of the many varieties here distinguished accord with the swings of business cycles. Group differences in this respect are less during contraction than during expansion. There is greater diversity of business fortunes, and of buyers' behavior, during business expansions than during contractions.

29) From a study of the order and the extent to which outlays of buyers for different kinds of goods pick up after contraction and depression, and decline after expansion and prosperity, the following conclusions emerge:

a) Between reference cycle stages VI and VIII, when the proportion of commodities marked by increasing outlays is at a minimum (about one-sixth of the commodities studied) the extent of the participation in the advance is below the general average for the products of heavy industries and for producer goods in general, above the general average for farm products, consumer goods, and nondurables.

b) In the final period of business contraction (between stages VIII and IX) declines in buyers' outlays still exceed advances, but the proportion of commodities for which buyers' outlays are expanding increases among all groups. In each of six categories—human consumption goods, consumer goods, nondurables, farm products, foods, and crop products—more than half of the commodities are marked by expanding monetary payments. The groups that take the lead in contributing to a business upturn in the terminal stages of general business recession are farm products and goods in shape for final purchase by consumers. In the primary farm markets and in the markets for finished consumer goods the forces of recovery are manifest while the tide of business at large is still ebbing.

c) The wide diversity of forces affecting business in the terminal period of cyclical contraction is evidenced by a range extending from 13 (the percentage of metals for which buyers' outlays increase) to 92 (the corresponding percentage of crop products).

d) Although rising demand for consumer goods and increasing revenues of farmers may play important roles in checking contraction and initiating recovery, the lead is quickly taken by other groups once the tide has turned. The striking shift in the spectrum of buyers' outlays as the trough of depression is passed is a notable feature of the present evidence. Durable goods and metals, least active positively between reference cycle stages VIII and IX, participate most completely in recovery between stages I and II, while consumer goods, crop products, and foods are lowest in percentage of outlay increases, once the turn has been rounded. This extraordinary reversal, as the center of business activity shifts from the farm and consumer sectors to the industrial, manufacturing, and producer goods sectors, is an obvious manifestation of a change in the business weather. It is no accident that business annals and the quantitative records of business activity place the upturn in business fortunes at the stage where this shift occurs.

e) The characteristic retardation of business expansion after reference stage II is reflected in 15 of the 16 commodity groups studied. This check is most marked among goods in the consumption, nondurable categories, goods much less subject to fluctuations during the full cycle than are products of heavy industry. Among the nondurables and consumption goods this early retardation is more pronounced at the manufacturing, producer goods stages than in the markets for finished consumer goods. The swing back after stage III is most marked, also, among manufactured goods and among the generally less sensitive consumption goods, nondurables, foods, and farm products.

f) Expanding activity is most pervasively characteristic of the economy between reference cycle stages III and IV. Not only is the percentage of participation in the expansion at a maximum, for all commodities studied, but the range of group differences, in percentage of commodities marked by increasing buyers' outlays, is at a minimum. This is a period of concerted, general advance in aggregate monetary payments for commodities.

g) In the final period of general expansion (between reference cycle stages IV and V), the proportion of commodities contributing to expansion in buyers' outlays is reduced for all groups except raw materials, the reduction being greatest for foods and consumer goods generally.

h) The abrupt reversal of the cyclical current after reference cycle stage V is accompanied by an extreme shrinkage in monetary payments for all classes of goods. With this shrinkage comes another revolutionary shift in the spectrum of buyers' outlays. Purchasing is curtailed throughout the economy, but in relative terms the focus shifts from the heavy industry, capital equipment, and durable goods sectors to the farm products, consumption goods, and nondurable sectors. In these latter groups resistance to the forces of recession is strongest. The relative advantage of consumption goods and nondurables is reduced during the next two periods (between reference cycle stages VI and VIII), as general contraction becomes more pervasive, and is then sharply increased in the terminal stages of contraction as the early pressures of recovery are felt in the markets for these goods. As they led in checking contraction, so do consumption goods, nondurables, and farm products lead in initiating recovery. Thereafter, as business at large passes the trough of depression at stage I of reference cycles, these are shouldered from the lead by durables, capital goods, nonfarm products, and producer goods.

30) These expansions and contractions in monetary payments reflect the combined influence of fluctuations in unit prices and in the quantity of goods changing hands. We summarize now

the roles of each factor in the cyclical movements of outlays and revenues for major classes of goods.

a) In the earliest manifestations of recovery in the consumer goods, farm products, and nondurable sectors (between reference cycle stages VI-VII and VII-VIII) increases in quantities are solely responsible for increases in the proportion of commodities showing outlay advances.

b) In the general reenforcing of incipient expansion in the farm products, consumption goods sectors during the final phase of contraction in business at large, and in the initiation of outlay increases for durables and industrial products generally, the quantity factor still plays a dominating role in all commodity groups. Price increases begin to supplement quantity gains, however, particularly among farm products, foods, and nondurables.

c) As the turn is rounded at stage IX of reference cycles, price becomes the dominant factor making for heavier monetary outlays by buyers of farm products, consumption goods, nondurables, and raw materials. This is the case, indeed, for 11 of our 16 groups. Thus early in business cycles there is manifest pressure on the supplies of certain classes of goods—goods whose supply cannot be expanded on short notice. For metals and other minerals, durable goods, capital equipment, and nonfarm products an increase in the quantity of goods changing hands is the chief factor making for heavier outlays.

d) In the pervasive check to expansion that comes after reference cycle stage II, quantities play a dominant role, forcing reductions in the scope of expansion for 10 of the 16 commodity groups. Prices exert a similar influence in 5 groups.

e) With the resumption of expansion in buyers' outlays after stage III, quantities play the chief part among animal products, consumption goods, and nondurables. Price advances are predominantly responsible for the increased scope of outlay increases among industrial products, durables, and capital equipment. Limits on volume expansion are being reached for industrial products and durables.

f) Restrictions on outlay increases in the final period of general business expansion (between stages IV and V) reflect price weakness among capital goods, nonfarm products, metals, and durable goods. The quantity factor is dominant in checking outlay increases among farm products, nondurables, and consumption goods generally.

g) As general business contraction develops after stage V prices reenforce quantities in a sharp curtailment of buyers' outlays, but quantity is the dominant factor for 13 of the 16 commodity groups. For foods alone is price clearly more potent than quantity in reducing the percentage of commodities for which outlays expand.

h) The leading depressant role passes to prices as the momentum of contraction gains between reference cycle stages VI and VII. The downward pressure from quantities is relaxed; for certain groups actual outlay increases result from advances in physical volume. With the passage to period VII-VIII, which we have already reviewed, amelioration continues; prices press downward, but less heavily, quantities press downward, but less generally than prices, and various shoots of recovery appear among physical volume records. As this movement spreads, and buyers' outlays expand in markets for a wide variety of commodities, the familiar pattern of recovery repeats itself in a new cycle.

◄ APPENDICES ►

APPENDIX TABLE 1

Commodities Used in the Study of Monetary Outlays and Price-Quantity Behavior in Business Cycles, and Specifications of Price and Quantity Series

The 64 paired price and quantity series entering into this study are described below. Characteristics of the sample are further indicated in Appendix Table 2, where group classifications are given. This note summarizes the specifications of the various series and calls attention to various limitations attaching to the sample and to the derived measures discussed in the text.

A considerable variety of commodities is covered, but the sample does not include in due proportion representatives of all the commodities produced and consumed in the United States. The make-up of the sample is suggested by the following tabulations.

	NO. OF COMMODITIES		NO. OF COMMODITIES
Raw materials	32	Producer goods (incl. 29 intended for human consumption)	48
Manufactured goods	32		
Total	64		
		Consumer goods	22
American farm products	33	Total	70 b
Other than American farm products	31	Goods intended for use in capital equipment and as building materials	21
Total	64		
Crop products, domestic	12	Producer fuels	6 a
Animal products, domestic	21	Goods intended for human consumption (incl. 24 foods)	49
Imported agricultural products	4 a		
Forest products	2 a	Total	76 b
Metal products	15	Durable goods	19
Nonmetallic minerals and their products	10	Nondurable goods	44
		Producer fuels	6 a
Total	64	Total	69 b

a Groups including less than 10 commodities are omitted from the group summaries and discussions in the text.
b Totals for these three classifications exceed 64 because certain commodities are included in more than one group: e.g., passenger automobiles are classified as both a producer and a consumer good.

Variations in the time coverage of the series are pronounced. For two commodities we have observations going back to 1858, covering 20 reference cycles. For three commodities the coverage is restricted to the three reference cycles that have run their course since 1924.

The other 59 commodities fall between these extremes. The observations are continuous from the dates of the first records through the 1938 trough, except for lumber, anthracite coal, and steel rails. The time coverage of each pair of series is indicated in this Appendix. A summary, by reference cycles, appears below. Here the unit of observation is the 'commodity-cycle'—a record for one commodity (more exactly, one pair of measures for a commodity) in one business cycle. There are 520 of these observations, divided in the manner indicated in the accompanying text. The

REFERENCE CYCLE	NO. OF COMMODITIES	REFERENCE CYCLE	NO. OF COMMODITIES	REFERENCE CYCLE	NO. OF COMMODITIES
1933-1938	62	1908-1912	26	1885-1888	8
1927-1933	63	1904-1908	22	1879-1885	7
1924-1927	62	1900-1904	21	1870-1879	4
1921-1924	60	1897-1900	19	1867-1870	2
1919-1921	58	1894-1897	16	1861-1867	2
1914-1919	36	1891-1894	15	1858-1861	2
1912-1914	27	1888-1891	8	Total	520

coverage approaches or exceeds 60 for each of the five cycles recorded since 1919. Of the 520 observations, 305 are for these five latest cycles. For earlier cycles there is a rather sharp falling off, with records for only two commodities for each of the three cycles between 1858 and 1870. This means that if the more recent cycles have had distinctive characteristics, different from those of earlier cycles, the aggregates will be disproportionately affected by the observations on recent cycles.

The series included differ materially in the markets represented by the price quotations and in the transactions represented by the quantity series. All prices are at wholesale, but there is latitude for considerable difference. Asphalt is quoted at refineries; cattle in Chicago markets; anthracite coal in New York Harbor; petroleum at wells in Pennsylvania; steel rails at mills in Pennsylvania. Differences in price behavior that may be commented upon in the text reflect these market differences as well as the obvious commodity differences. There are even wider differences among the series of physical quantities used. These fall into 8 general categories.

Production	28
Consumption of materials in productive processes	10
Consumption of animal food products ready for use	3
Shipments and receipts	14
Exports (raw cotton)	1
Imports	4
New orders	3
Factory sales (passenger automobiles)	1
Total	64

This heterogeneity places limitations on any generalizations based on aggregates. The cyclical behavior of quantity series for two commodities may differ because of industrial differences, differences in degree of fabrication or coverage, or because one series is for output at the mill while another is for exports.[1]

Finally, we note problems concerning the pairing of individual price and quantity series. The ideal, for present purposes, would be price quotations and quantity records relating to precisely the same transactions, and with no time lag between the quoting of the price, the delivery of the goods, and the transfer of the funds in payment. In some cases these requirements are approximated fairly closely. For raw milk New York prices are used, and the quantity series defines fluid milk receipts in the same market. Time lags between price quotation, delivery of milk, and transfer of funds are well within the interval represented by a stage in a given reference cycle —the shortest time unit for which measures have been computed in this study. But for many of our commodity series the data fall far short of the requirements of the ideal situation. For men's shoes we pair the price of a particular type with production records for all varieties. In one petroleum combination we use the price of crude petroleum at Pennsylvania wells with total production of crude domestic petroleum. The Chicago price of potatoes is paired with total United States shipments. In a few cases, in default of better combinations, the output of a commodity closely related to that for which price is quoted is used as the quantity series (e.g., steel ingot production is paired with the price of steel scrap; deliveries of raw silk are paired with the price of silk yarn). For many of the metal series, and some others, a substantial proportion of total sales is made at contract prices holding for a season; quoted prices are for only a portion of total deliveries.

Other imperfections of pairing will be obvious to the reader who consults the details of this Appendix. Some are more serious than others. There are geographical differences in absolute prices, but for most commodities the movements of relative prices (which are here used) are similar in different parts of the country. Again, price changes for one representative of a family of commodities (e.g., one type of men's shoes) usually parallel changes in the prices of other

[1] The one export series we used—for raw cotton—is not strictly comparable with domestic production or consumption series, but it has sufficient importance for the domestic economy to warrant inclusion.

members. But the discrepancy between contract and quoted prices may impart a real bias to the record we have used, and it is a bias impossible to evaluate without access to private account books. Similarly, the pairing of price and quantity series relating to slightly different processed forms leaves the way open for inaccuracies. For these various reasons we must regard some of our patterns of related price-quantity changes in business cycles as rough approximations, open to substantial improvement in later studies.

Our estimates of monetary outlays on the part of buyers are subject to a margin of error in certain cases, also, because of possible timing differences between the quoting of prices and the delivery of goods, and between delivery and payment. Such errors are lessened by the use of stages of reference cycles, not months, as the time unit. The shortest interstage interval, as averaged for the period of this study, covers over three months (the average interval between reference cycle stages V and VI). For most commodity transactions the lag of payments behind deliveries is well within this margin. The assumption that physical deliveries and monetary payments are synchronous, within the time units here employed, is probably not seriously in error. Greater errors may result from the assumption that quoted prices and records of production (or consumption, or delivery), as compiled by federal and other agencies, relate to synchronous events. Here, again, we must trust to the averaging process involved in the use of reference cycle stages as time units to eliminate some of the timing discrepancies due to this assumption.

The commodities employed in this study, with the periods covered by the price and quantity series paired in each case, and the specifications of the series, are given below. The parenthetical figure after each commodity indicates the number of reference cycles covered. All prices are for transactions at wholesale. The abbreviations are:

BAE: United States Bureau of Agricultural Economics
BLS: United States Bureau of Labor Statistics
Census: United States Bureau of the Census
Commerce: United States Bureau of Foreign and Domestic Commerce
Mines: United States Bureau of Mines
NBER: National Bureau of Economic Research
† Seasonally corrected.

Asphalt, 1919-38 (5)
Price: Dollars per short ton, bulk, at refineries
Source: BLS
†Quantity: Production, short tons. Production data are for asphalt derived from domestic and foreign petroleum, the larger proportion from foreign petroleum, mainly Mexican. Native asphalt is excluded.
Source: Mines

Automobiles, passenger, 1914-38 (6)
Price: Index on 1926 base. For 1913-26 the index is a weighted average of 6 makes of passenger cars (Buick, Cadillac, Chevrolet, Dodge, Ford, and Packard). For 1926-38, 3 types of chassis (4-door, 2-door, and coupe) are used instead of 1.
Source: BLS
†Quantity: Factory sales, number
Source: 1914-21, National Automobile Chamber of Commerce; 1921-38, Census

Beef, 1919-38 (5)
†Price: Cents per lb., New York, fresh
Source: BLS
†Quantity: Consumption of beef and veal, lbs.
Source: BAE

Bread, 1914-38 (6)
Price: Cents per lb., New York, white
Source: BLS
†Quantity: Production of wheat flour. See Flour (combination 1)

Butter (combination 1), 1919-38 (5)
†Price: See Butter (combination 2)
†Quantity: Production in factories, lbs.
Source: BAE

Butter (combination 2), 1912-38 (7)
†Price: Cents per lb., Chicago, creamery extra
Source: BLS
†Quantity: Receipts at 5 markets, lbs.
Source: BAE

Cattle (combination 1), 1858-1938 (20)
†Price: Dollars per 100 lbs., Chicago
Source: 1858-99, Chicago Board of Trade; 1900-38, BAE
†Quantity: Receipts, number, Chicago
Source: Chicago Board of Trade
Value series for cattle is derived from price per pound and number of animals. The assumption is implicit that animals marketed did not change in average weight in the course of any given business cycle.

Cattle (combination 2), 1908-38 (8)
†Price: See Cattle (combination 1)
†Quantity: Slaughtered under federal inspection, number
Source: BAE
See under Cattle (combination 1) note concerning value

Cement, 1914-38 (6)
Price: Dollars per bbl., cars, Chicago
Source: *Engineering News-Record*
†Quantity: Production, bbls.
Source: 1914-21, Portland Cement Association; 1921-38, Mines

Coal, anthracite, 1891-97, 1908-12, 1914-21, 1927-38 (7 cycles excl. periods affected by strikes)
†Price: Dollars per long ton; 1891-1924, New York Harbor; 1924-38, composite price at 8 cities; chestnut, seasonally corrected 1901-38
Source: BLS
†Quantity: 1891-1919, shipments, long tons; 1919-38, production, short tons; Pennsylvania
Source: 1891-1919, Bureau of Anthracite Coal Statistics; 1919-38, Mines

Coal, bituminous, 1908-38 (8)
†Price: Dollars per short ton; 1908-24, mine run; 1924-38, f.o.b. mines, composite price; seasonally corrected for 1908-29
Source: 1908-24, Mines; 1924-38, BLS
†Quantity: Production, short tons
Source: Mines

Coffee, 1891-1938 (13)
Price: Cents per lb., New York, Rio, #7
Source: BLS
†Quantity: Imports, lbs.
Source: Commerce

Coke, beehive, 1897-1938 (11)
Price: Dollars per short ton, Connellsville furnace
Source: BLS
†Quantity: Production, short tons
Source: Mines

Copper, 1919-38 (5)
Price: Cents per lb., New York, electrolytic
Source: Engineering and Mining Journal
†Quantity: Refined production, North and South America, short tons
Source: 1919-24, Copper Export Association; 1924-38, American Bureau of Metal Statistics

Corn, 1919-38 (5)
†Price: Dollars per bu., Chicago, contract grades or better
Source: Chicago Board of Trade
†Quantity: Grindings, bu., grinding of corn by wet process in manufacture of cornstarch, glucose, etc.
Source: Corn Industries Research Foundation

Cotton, raw (combination 1), 1914-38 (6)
†Price: See Cotton, raw (combination 2)
†Quantity: Consumption, running bales
Source: Census

Cotton, raw (combination 2), 1870-1938 (17)
†Price: Cents per lb., New York, middling upland
Source: 1870-89, Cotton Facts, Shepperson; 1890-1938, BLS
†Quantity: Exports, lbs.
Source: Commerce

Cotton, yarn, 1914-38 (6)
Price: Cents per lb., mill, carded, northern, cones 10/1
Source: BLS

Cotton, yarn (cont.)
†Quantity: See Cotton, raw (combination 1)

Cottonseed oil, crude, 1919-38 (5)
Price: Cents per lb., f.o.b. southeastern mills
Source: BAE
†Quantity: Production, lbs.
Source: Census

Cottonseed oil, refined, 1919-38 (5)
Price: Cents per lb., New York, prime, summer, yellow
Source: 1919-33, BAE; 1933-38, BLS
†Quantity: Production, lbs.
Source: Census

Eggs, 1912-38 (7)
†Price: Cents per doz., New York, firsts
Source: BLS
†Quantity: Receipts, cases of 30 doz.; 1910-19, 7 markets; 1919-38, 5 markets
Source: BAE

Flour (combination 1), 1914-38 (6)
Price: See Flour (combination 2)
†Quantity: Production of wheat flour, bbls.
Source: 1914-24, A. L. Russell; 1924-38, Food Research Institute

Flour (combination 2), 1891-1938 (13)
Price: Dollars per bbl.; 1891-1914, New York, spring patents; 1914-38, Minneapolis, standard patents
Source: BLS
†Quantity: Shipments, bbls., Minneapolis. This represents about 10 percent of United States production.
Source: Minneapolis Chamber of Commerce

Gasoline, 1919-38 (5)
†Price: Cents per gal., Pennsylvania refineries
Source: BLS
†Quantity: Refinery production, bbls.
Source: Mines

Glass, plate, 1924-38 (3)
Price: Cents per sq. ft., New York
Source: BLS

Glass, plate (*cont.*)
†Quantity: Production, sq. ft.
  Source: Plate Glass Manufacturers
  of America

Hides, 1921-38 (4)
†Price: Cents per lb., Chicago, pack-
  ers, heavy, native steers
  Source: BLS
†Quantity: Total movement into sight,
  number
  Source: Tanners' Council of America
Value series for hides is derived from
price per pound and number of
skins. The assumption is implicit
that skins marketed did not change
in average weight in the course of
any given business cycle.

Hogs (combination 1), 1858-1938 (20)
†Price: Dollars per 100 lbs., Chicago,
  heavy
  Source: Chicago Board of Trade
†Quantity: Receipts, number, Chi-
  cago
  Source: Chicago Board of Trade
See under Cattle (combination 1)
note concerning value

Hogs (combination 2), 1879-1938 (16)
†Price: See Hogs (combination 1)
†Quantity: 1879-1906, commercial
  slaughter estimated by the Bureau of Agricultural Economics on
  the basis of total eastern and western slaughter as reported by *The
  Price Current Yearbook* and monthly slaughter computed on basis of
  western slaughter and receipts at
  markets; 1907-38, slaughtered under federal inspection; number
  Source: BAE
See under Cattle (combination 1)
note concerning value

Iron ore, 1919-38 (5)
Price: Dollars per long ton, delivered
  to lower lake ports, Mesabi Non-
  Bessemer
  Source: *Steel*
†Quantity: Consumption by furnaces
  (incl. Canada) of Lake Superior
  ore, long tons
  Source: Lake Superior Iron Ore
  Association

Lard, 1919-38 (5)
†Price: Cents per lb., New York, prime
  contract
  Source: BLS
†Quantity: Production from federally
  inspected slaughter, lbs.
  Source: BAE

Lead, ore, 1897-1938 (11)
Price: Cents per lb., New York
  Source: *Engineering and Mining
  Journal*
†Quantity: Shipments, short tons,
  Joplin District
  Source: 1895-1903, *Engineering and
  Mining Journal*; 1903-38, New York
  Metal Exchange

Leather, 1921-38 (4)
Price: Cents per lb., Boston, sole
  oak, scoured backs
  Source: BLS
†Quantity: Production of cattle hide
  leathers and kip leathers, equiv-
  alent hides
  Source: Tanners' Council of America
See under Hides note concerning
value

Linseed oil, 1919-38 (5)
Price: Cents per gal., raw, New York
  Source: BLS
†Quantity: Production, lbs., quarterly
  data
  Source: Census

Lubricants, 1919-38 (5)
Price: Cents per gal., refineries, Penn-
  sylvania
  Source: BLS
†Quantity: Production, bbls.
  Source: Mines

Lumber, Douglas fir, 1919-33 (4)
Price: Dollars per M bd. ft., Port-
  land mills
  Source: BLS
†Quantity: Production, bd. ft.
  Source: West Coast Lumbermen's
  Association

Meat, 1919-38 (5)
Price: Index on 1926 base; includes beef, veal, lamb, mutton, pork, lard
Source: NBER
†Quantity: Consumption, lbs.; includes production of beef, veal, lamb, mutton, pork, lard, computed from federal inspected slaughter, plus imports, minus exports and the change in cold storage holdings
Source: BAE

Milk, condensed, 1919-38 (5)
Price: Dollars per case, 48 fourteen oz. cans, New York
Source: BLS
†Quantity: Production of sweetened condensed milk, case goods, lbs.
Source: BAE

Milk, evaporated, 1919-38 (5)
Price: Dollars per case, 48 fourteen and one-half oz. cans, New York
Source: BLS
†Quantity: Production, case goods, lbs.
Source: BAE

Milk, raw, 1894-1938 (12)
†Price: Dollars per 100 lbs., New York, fresh, seasonally corrected 1891-1924
Source: BLS
†Quantity: Receipts of fluid milk, New York market, cans of 40 qts.
Source: BAE

Paper, 1919-38 (5)
Price: Index on 1926 base; includes boxboard, book paper, newsprint, tissue, and wrapping paper
Source: NBER
†Quantity: Production of all grades of paper, short tons
Source: Federal Trade Commission

Petroleum (combination 1), 1891-1938 (13)
Price: Dollars per bbl., crude at wells, Pennsylvania
Source: BLS
†Quantity: Production of Appalachian field, bbls. The Appalachian

Petroleum (combination 1) (cont.)
field represented 50 percent of production in 1900, 4 percent in 1924, because of the rapid development of mid-continental and California fields.
Source: Mines

Petroleum (combination 2), 1914-38 (6)
Price: See Petroleum (combination 1)
†Quantity: Production of crude domestic petroleum, bbls.
Source: Mines

Pig iron (combination 1), 1904-38 (9)
Price: Dollars per long ton, composite consisting of four quotations: Bessemer, Pittsburgh, 1891-1938; Foundry #1, Philadelphia, 1891-1914; Basic, 1914-38; Foundry #2, northern, Pittsburgh, 1891-1938; Gray Forge, southern, Cincinnati, 1891-1914; Foundry #2, southern, Cincinnati, 1914-21; Foundry #2, southern, Birmingham, 1921-38
Source: NBER
†Quantity: Production at merchant furnaces, long tons
Source: *Iron Age*

Pig iron (combination 2), 1879-1938 (16)
Price: Dollars per long ton; 1879-1912, #1 Anthracite foundry; 1912-38, Eastern Pennsylvania
Source: American Iron and Steel Institute
†Quantity: Production, long tons
Source: *Iron Age*

Pork, 1919-38 (5)
†Price: Index on 1926 base of pork products (fresh and cured) and lard
Source: NBER
†Quantity: Consumption of pork products, incl. lard, lbs.
Source: BAE

Potatoes, 1919-38 (5)
†Price: Dollars per 100 lbs., Chicago
Source: BLS

Potatoes (cont.)
†Quantity: Shipments, bu., carlots
Source: BAE

Rubber, 1891-1938 (13)
Price: Cents per lb., New York; 1891-1914, Para, island; 1914-38, Plantation
Source: BLS
†Quantity: Imports, lbs.
Source: Commerce

Sheep (combination 1), 1879-1938 (16)
†Price: Dollars per 100 lbs., Chicago
Source: 1879-1904, Chicago Board of Trade; 1905-40, BAE
†Quantity: Receipts of sheep and lambs, number, Chicago
Source: Chicago Board of Trade
See under Cattle (combination 1) note concerning value

Sheep (combination 2), 1908-38 (8)
†Price: See Sheep (combination 1)
†Quantity: Slaughter of sheep and lambs under federal inspection, number
Source: BAE
See under Cattle (combination 1) note concerning value

Shoes, 1924-38 (3)
Price: Dollars per pair, factory, men's, black vici kid, Goodyear welt
Source: BLS
†Quantity: Production of men's shoes, pairs
Source: Census

Silk, raw, 1891-1938 (13)
†Price: Dollars per lb., New York, Japanese; 1891-1919, filatures; 1919-38, white 78 percent, 13/15 denier, double extra crack
Source: BLS
†Quantity: Imports, lbs.
Source: Commerce

Silk, yarn, 1921-38 (4)
Price: Dollars per lb., New York, spun, domestic, gray, 60/2
Source: BLS
†Quantity: Deliveries of raw silk to mills, bales

Silk, yarn (cont.)
Source: 1921-29, Textile Economics Bureau, Inc.; 1929-38, Commodity Exchange, Inc.

Steel billets, 1900-38 (10)
Price: Dollars per long ton, Pittsburgh, Bessemer
Source: BLS
†Quantity: Production of steel ingots, long tons
Source: Iron Age

Steel plates, 1924-38 (3)
Price: Cents per lb., Pittsburgh, tank
Source: Iron Age
Quantity: New orders, short tons, fabricated
Source: Census

Steel rails, 1870-1924 (14)
Price: Dollars per long ton, mills, Pennsylvania; 1870-1919, Bessemer; 1919-24, open hearth; heavy standard
Source: Iron Age
†Quantity: Orders by railroads, long tons, quarterly data
Source: Railroad Purchasing and the Business Cycle, Partington

Steel scrap, 1900-38 (10)
†Price: Dollars per long ton, Chicago, heavy melting, #1
Source: Iron Age
†Quantity: See under Steel billets, ingot production

Steel sheets, 1919-38 (5)
Price: Cents per lb., Pittsburgh, box, annealed, #27
Source: BLS
†Quantity: Production, short tons; 1933-38, quarterly data
Source: 1919-33, National Association of Flat Rolled Steel Manufacturers; 1933-38, American Iron and Steel Institute

Steel, structural, 1914-38 (6)
Price: Dollars per 100 lbs., mill, Pittsburgh, shapes, beams, etc., 3" and larger
Source: BLS

Steel, structural *(cont.)*
†Quantity: New orders, short tons, fabricated
Source: American Iron and Steel Institute

Sugar, 1891-1938 (13)
†Price: Cents per lb., granulated, New York, seasonally corrected 1891-1911
Source: BLS
†Quantity: Meltings, long tons; 1891-1921, at 4 ports; 1921-38, at 8 ports
Source: *Weekly Statistical Sugar Trade Journal*

Tin, 1885-1938 (15)
Price: Cents per lb., New York, Straits tin
Source: 1885-99, *Mineral Industry*; 1900-38, *Metal Statistics*
Quantity: Imports, long tons
Source: Commerce

Wool, raw, 1919-38 (5)
Price: Cents per lb., Boston, Ohio, fine clothing
Source: BLS

Wool, raw *(cont.)*
†Quantity: Consumption, lbs., scoured basis
Source: Census

Worsted yarn, 1919-38 (5)
Price: Dollars per lb., mill, 2/40 half blood
Source: BLS
†Quantity: Consumption of apparel class wool, lbs., scoured basis
Source: Census

Zinc, raw, 1897-1938 (11)
†Price: Cents per lb., New York, slab
Source: *Iron Age*
†Quantity: Shipments of zinc ore, Joplin District, short tons
Source: 1897-1903, *Engineering and Mining Journal*; 1904-21, New York Metal Exchange; 1921-38, *Joplin Globe*

Zinc, sheet, 1897-1938 (11)
Price: Dollars per 100 lbs., LaSalle, Ill.
Source: BLS
†Quantity: See Zinc, raw

APPENDIX TABLE 2

Composition of Commodity Groups

In interpreting the various descriptive measures of commodity groups given in the text, the reader should understand that these groups vary considerably in degree of representativeness. We estimate that the over-all sample includes, directly or by imputation, about one-third, by value, of the agricultural products, raw minerals, and manufactured goods produced in the United States in 1937. Corresponding percentages for the separate groups cover a wide range. These differences are indicated in the summary that follows, in which certain characteristics of the several commodity groups are briefly noted. The numbers in parentheses indicate the number of price and quantity combinations used for commodities that appear more than once.

Raw materials. This sample is the most representative in our list. The commodities included are coffee, corn, crude cottonseed oil, potatoes, cattle (2), hogs (2), sheep (2), eggs, raw milk, hides, raw cotton (2), raw silk, raw wool, anthracite and bituminous coal, petroleum (2), iron ore, pig iron (2), steel scrap, copper, lead, tin, zinc, lumber (fir), linseed oil, rubber. They amount in value to about three-quarters of all raw materials produced in 1937. The chief gaps are in fruits and vegetables, grains (among which corn alone is included), and lumber (fir alone being included).

Manufactured goods. This sample comprehends, directly or by imputation, about one-fifth, by value, of manufactured goods produced in 1937. The commodities included are bread, butter (2), refined cottonseed oil, flour (2), beef, lard, pork products, meat index (including beef, pork, lamb, mutton, veal, lard), condensed and evaporated milk, sugar, cotton yarn, silk yarn, worsted yarn, leather, men's shoes, coke, gasoline, lubricants, steel billets, steel plates, steel rails, steel sheet, structural steel, zinc sheet, passenger automobiles, asphalt, cement, plate glass, paper index (including boxboard, book, newsprint, tissue, wrapping). The chief gaps are in manufactured foods, cloths and clothing, forest products, printing and publishing, chemicals and allied products, stone, clay and glass products, rubber products, finished iron and steel products, nonferrous metals and their products, machinery, transportation equipment. The sample is broad enough to give results that are suggestive, but no more.

Products of American farms. This sample, covering some 50 percent, by value, of agricultural commodities produced in 1937, includes bread, corn, cottonseed oil (2), flour (2), potatoes, sugar, cattle (2), hogs (2), sheep (2), butter (2), eggs, milk (3), beef, pork products, lard, meat index, hides, leather, men's shoes, cotton (3), wool (2), linseed oil. The chief gaps are in grains, cheese, tobacco, poultry, fruits and vegetables, cereals, cloths and clothing.

Crop products. The commodities included are bread, corn, cottonseed oil (2), potatoes, flour (2), sugar, cotton (3), linseed oil.

Animal products. The commodities included are butter (2), cattle (2), hogs (2), sheep (2), eggs, milk (3), hides, leather, men's shoes, beef, lard, pork products, meat index, wool (2).

Goods other than products of American farms. In this group we include about one-quarter, by value, of nonfarm commodities produced in 1937. The commodities represented are coffee, silk (2), anthracite and bituminous coal, coke, petroleum (2), gasoline, lubricants, iron ore, pig iron (2), steel scrap, steel billets, steel plates, steel rails, steel sheet, structural steel, copper, lead, tin, zinc (2), passenger automobiles, asphalt, cement, plate glass, lumber (fir), paper index, rubber. The chief gaps are in forest products, printing and publishing, chemicals and allied products, rubber products, stone, clay and glass products, highly fabricated iron and steel products, nonferrous metals and their products, machinery, transportation equipment.

Metals. The commodities included are iron ore, pig iron (2), steel scrap, steel billets, steel plates, steel rails, steel sheets, structural steel, copper, lead, tin, zinc (2), passenger automobiles.

Nonmetallic minerals. The commodities included are anthracite and bituminous coal, coke, gasoline, lubricants, petroleum (2), asphalt, cement, plate glass.

Producer goods, all. This sample, covering about one-fifth, by value, of such commodities produced in 1937, includes corn, cottonseed oil (2), flour (2), cattle (2), hogs (2), sheep (2), hides, leather, cotton (3), wool (2), silk (2), bituminous coal, coke, petroleum (2), gasoline, lubricants, iron ore, pig iron (2), steel scrap, steel billets, steel plates, steel rails, steel sheet, structural steel, copper, lead, tin, zinc (2), passenger automobiles, asphalt, cement, linseed oil, lumber (fir), plate glass, paper index, rubber. The chief gaps are in forest products, chemicals and allied products, rubber products, stone, clay and glass products, highly fabricated iron and steel manufactures, nonferrous metals and their products, machinery, transportation equipment.

Producer goods for human consumption. The commodities represented are corn, cottonseed oil (2), flour (2), cattle (2), hogs (2), sheep (2), hides, leather, cotton (3), silk (2), wool (2), petroleum (2), iron ore, pig iron (2), copper, lumber (fir), paper index, rubber.

Consumer goods. This sample, covering about half, by value, of consumer goods produced in 1937, includes bread, coffee, flour (2), potatoes, sugar, butter (2), eggs, milk (3), beef, lard, pork products, meat index, men's shoes, anthracite coal, coke (consumers' portion), gasoline, lubricants, passenger automobiles. The chief gaps are in manufactured foods, tobacco, drugs and household medicines, toilet preparations, books and newspapers, toys, games and sport supplies, illuminating and lighting materials and fixtures, cloths and clothing, house furnishings and equipment, heating and cooking apparatus, electrical home appliances, china and glassware, radio, phonograph and musical instruments, clocks and watches, tires, and rubber products.

Goods intended for use in capital equipment or as building materials. This sample is relatively small, including about one-tenth, by value, of commodities of this type produced in 1937. The commodities represented are iron ore, pig iron (2), steel scrap, steel billets, steel plates, steel rails, steel sheet, structural steel, copper, lead, tin, zinc (2), passenger automobiles, asphalt, cement, plate glass, linseed oil, lumber (fir), rubber. The chief gaps are in agricultural and industrial machinery, tools, textile machinery, nonferrous metals and their products, heavy electrical equipment, paint materials, plumbing and heating materials, lumber, trucks and transportation equipment, stone, clay and glass products.

Human consumption goods (i.e., goods, at various stages of fabrication, intended for ultimate human consumption). This sample, covering more than a third, by value, of commodities of this type produced in 1937, includes bread, coffee, corn, cottonseed oil (2), flour (2), potatoes, sugar, cattle (2), hogs (2), sheep (2), butter (2), eggs, milk (3), beef, lard, pork products, meat index, hides, leather, men's shoes, cotton (3), wool (2), silk (2), anthracite coal, coke (consumers' portion), petroleum (2), gasoline, lubricants, iron ore, pig iron (2), copper, passenger automobiles, lumber (fir), paper index, rubber. The chief gaps are in grains, poultry, fruits and vegetables (except potatoes), beverages, cereal products, wood pulp, books and magazines, cloths and clothing, gas and electricity, furniture and furnishings, household electrical appliances, tires and tubes.

Foods. This group, covering about 40 percent, by value, of foods produced in 1937, includes bread, coffee, corn, refined cottonseed oil, flour (2), potatoes, sugar, cattle (2), hogs (2), sheep (2), butter (2), eggs, milk (3), beef, lard, pork products, meat index. The chief gaps are in fish, cheese, ice cream, poultry, sausage meats, fruits and vegetables, cereals, chocolate and cocoa, beverages.

Durable goods. The sample covers about one-tenth, by value, of durable goods produced in 1937; it includes iron ore, pig iron (2), steel scrap, steel billets, steel plates, steel rails, steel sheet, structural steel, copper, lead, tin, zinc (2), passenger automobiles, asphalt, cement, plate glass, lumber (fir). The chief gaps are in forest products, stone, clay and glass products, highly fabricated iron and steel products, nonferrous metals and their products, machinery, transportation equipment.

Nondurable goods. This sample, covering about two-fifths, by value, of nondurables produced in 1937, includes bread, coffee, corn, cottonseed oil (2), flour (2), potatoes, sugar, cattle (2), hogs (2), sheep (2), butter (2), eggs, milk (3), beef, lard, pork products, meat index, hides, leather, men's shoes, cotton (3), wool (2), silk (2), anthracite coal, coke, petroleum (2), gasoline, lubricants, linseed oil, paper index, rubber. The chief gaps are in manufactured foods, cloths and clothing, printing and publishing, chemicals and allied products, rubber products, tobacco.

APPENDIX TABLE 3

Average Movements of Aggregate Values, Average Unit Prices, and Physical Volumes, in Business Cycles
All Commodities and Sixteen Major Commodity Groups

	REFERENCE CYCLE STAGES								
	I	II	III	IV	V	VI	VII	VIII	IX
All commodities									
Value	85	97	105	118	125	116	99	85	85
Price	94	99	104	110	112	110	99	91	90
Quantity	90	98	101	108	112	107	99	94	94
Raw materials									
Value	85	97	104	118	127	118	99	86	86
Price	92	99	104	112	115	112	99	90	89
Quantity	91	98	101	107	111	107	100	95	95
Manufactured goods									
Value	86	97	106	117	124	113	98	85	84
Price	96	100	104	107	110	108	100	92	91
Quantity	90	98	102	110	114	106	98	92	93
American farm products									
Value	94	103	105	115	119	112	97	89	91
Price	96	102	106	111	113	110	98	90	90
Quantity	98	101	99	103	105	102	99	99	100
Other than American farm products									
Value	77	91	104	121	132	121	100	81	79
Price	92	97	102	108	112	109	101	92	90
Quantity	82	95	104	114	120	112	100	88	87
Crop products, domestic									
Value	95	104	104	116	121	113	95	88	91
Price	96	102	106	112	114	112	94	87	89
Quantity	100	101	99	104	106	102	101	101	102
Animal products, domestic									
Value	93	102	105	114	117	111	99	90	90
Price	96	101	107	110	112	110	100	92	91
Quantity	97	101	99	103	105	101	98	98	99
Metals									
Value	70	89	106	127	140	124	99	77	72
Price	91	95	100	108	113	110	102	94	92
Quantity	76	94	107	120	126	115	98	82	79
Nonmetallic minerals									
Value	78	88	99	115	126	121	106	86	84
Price	91	96	101	106	109	108	101	93	90
Quantity	85	92	99	108	116	113	105	92	93

Appendix Table 3 *(concl.)*

	I	II	III	IV	V	VI	VII	VIII	IX
			REFERENCE CYCLE STAGES						
Producer goods, all									
Value	81	96	105	121	130	118	98	83	81
Price	93	99	104	110	114	110	99	91	89
Quantity	87	97	102	111	116	109	100	92	91
Producer goods for human consumption									
Value	87	99	106	120	127	117	97	86	85
Price	94	101	106	113	115	111	98	89	88
Quantity	92	99	101	107	111	106	100	96	96
Consumer goods									
Value	93	98	103	112	116	111	100	90	92
Price	97	100	104	107	109	108	100	92	91
Quantity	97	99	100	104	107	103	100	97	100
Capital equipment									
Value	75	92	106	125	138	123	98	79	75
Price	94	97	102	108	112	110	100	93	91
Quantity	79	95	105	117	125	114	99	84	82
Human consumption goods									
Value	89	99	105	116	123	115	99	87	87
Price	95	100	105	110	113	110	99	90	89
Quantity	94	99	100	106	109	105	100	96	97
Foods									
Value	96	101	104	112	113	109	100	93	96
Price	97	100	105	110	111	110	100	92	92
Quantity	100	101	99	102	102	100	100	102	104
Durable goods									
Value	73	90	106	125	137	123	99	78	74
Price	93	97	101	108	112	109	101	94	92
Quantity	78	94	106	119	125	114	99	83	81
Nondurable goods									
Value	91	100	104	115	120	113	98	89	90
Price	95	101	106	110	113	110	99	90	89
Quantity	96	100	99	104	107	103	99	99	100

Changes in Proportion of Commodities Marked by Increases in Buyers' Outlays between Successive Stages of Business Cycles, by Commodity Groups

Percentage of commodities in group showing increases in outlays, with division into price-dominated and quantity-dominated classes

The figures in the two columns of price and quantity dominance define the percentages of the total number of commodities in each group showing increases in buyers' outlays due predominantly to price increases and to quantity increases. The sum of the two percentages, for a given commodity group, is the total percentage of commodities in that group showing outlay increases in the stated interstage period. The difference between this total and 100 is the percentage of commodities showing outlay decreases, or no change in outlay.

INTERSTAGE PERIOD VII-VIII

	TOTAL	PRICES DOMINANT	QUANTITIES DOMINANT
Crop products, domestic	33	0	33
Consumer goods	32	0	32
Foods	29	0	29
Am. farm products	24	0	24
Nondurable goods	23	0	23
Consumption goods	20	0	20
Animal products, domestic	19*	0	19
Manufactured goods	19	0	19
All commodities	17	0	17
Raw materials	16*	0	16
Producer goods for human consumption	14	0	14
Capital equipment	10	0	10
Non-Am. farm products	10*	0	10
Nonmetallic minerals	10*	0	10
Producer goods, all	10*	0	10
Durable goods	5*	0	5
Metals	0*	0	0

INTERSTAGE PERIOD VIII-IX

	TOTAL	PRICES DOMINANT	QUANTITIES DOMINANT
Crop products, domestic	92	29	63
Foods	63	13	50
Am. farm products	61	17	44
Consumer goods	59	9	50
Nondurable goods	56	12	44
Consumption goods	51	11	40
Producer goods for human consumption	48	12	36
Manufactured goods	47	9	38
All commodities	45	9	36
Animal products, domestic	43	10	33
Raw materials	43	9	34
Producer goods, all	37	8	29
Nonmetallic minerals	30	5	25
Non-Am. farm products	29	2	27
Capital equipment	24	2	22
Durable goods	21	3	18
Metals	13	0	13

INTERSTAGE PERIOD I-II

	TOTAL	PRICES DOMINANT	QUANTITIES DOMINANT
Durable goods	100	16	84
Metals	100	13	87
Capital equipment	95	19	76
Non-Am. farm products	94	26	68
Producer goods, all	94	38	56
Nonmetallic minerals	90	30	60
Producer goods for human consumption	89	48	41
Raw materials	88	41	47
All commodities	84	34	50
Animal products, domestic	81	38	43
Manufactured goods	81	28	53
Consumption goods	80	41	39
Nondurable goods	77	43	34
Am. farm products	75	42	33
Crop products, domestic	67	50	17
Foods	67	42	25
Consumer goods	64	32	32

INTERSTAGE PERIOD II-III

	TOTAL	PRICES DOMINANT	QUANTITIES DOMINANT
Durable goods	95	19	76
Metals	93	17	76
Nonmetallic minerals	90	50	40
Non-Am. farm products	87	27	60
Capital equipment	86	17	69
Producer goods, all	69	30	39
Raw materials	66	31	35
All commodities	64	27	37
Manufactured goods	62	23	39
Consumption goods	58	29	29
Producer goods for human consumption	58	31	27
Consumer goods	55	23	32
Foods	50	29	21
Nondurable goods	50	30	20
Animal products, domestic	43	38	5
Am. farm products	42	27	15
Crop products, domestic	41	8	33

APPENDIX TABLE 4 *(concl.)*

INTERSTAGE PERIOD III-IV

	TOTAL	PRICES DOMINANT	QUANTITIES DOMINANT
Durable goods	100	39	61
Metals	100	40	60
Nonmetallic minerals	100	45	55
Non-Am. farm products	97	40	57
Capital equipment	95	36	59
Manufactured goods	94	31	63
Producer goods, all	92	39	53
All commodities	*89*	*37*	*52*
Producer goods for human consumption	89	41	48
Foods	88	40	48
Consumption goods	88	38	50
Consumer goods	86	34	52
Raw materials	85	44	41
Crop products, domestic	84	46	38
Nondurable goods	84	37	47
Am. farm products	82	35	47
Animal products, domestic	80	28	52

INTERSTAGE PERIOD IV-V

	TOTAL	PRICES DOMINANT	QUANTITIES DOMINANT
Capital equipment	90	19	71
Nonmetallic minerals	90	20	70
Durable goods	89	21	68
Non-Am. farm products	88	26	62
Producer goods for human consumption	88	43	45
Metals	87	20	67
Producer goods, all	86	34	52
Raw materials	86	36	50
All commodities	*80*	*32*	*48*
Consumption goods	77	36	41
Nondurable goods	76	37	39
Crop products, domestic	75	42	33
Manufactured goods	75	28	47
Am. farm products	74	38	36
Animal products, domestic	74	36	38
Foods	69	44	25
Consumer goods	63	27	36

INTERSTAGE PERIOD V-VI

	TOTAL	PRICES DOMINANT	QUANTITIES DOMINANT
Foods	46	25	21
Consumer goods	45	27	18
Animal products, domestic	43	19	24
Nonmetallic minerals	40	20	20
Am. farm products	33	18	15
Nondurable goods	30	16	14
Consumption goods	26	14	12
Manufactured goods	26	13	13
All commodities	*23*	*12*	*11*
Raw materials	21	12	9
Crop products, domestic	16	16	0
Non-Am. farm products	12	6	6
Producer goods, all	12	4	8
Producer goods for human consumption	11	4	7
Capital equipment	5*	0	5
Durable goods	5*	0	5
Metals	0*	0	0

INTERSTAGE PERIOD VI-VII

	TOTAL	PRICES DOMINANT	QUANTITIES DOMINANT
Nonmetallic minerals	30	10	20
Consumer goods	25*	8	17
Foods	23*	3	20
Animal products, domestic	19*	0	19
Am. farm products	17*	1	16
Manufactured goods	17*	1	16
Nondurable goods	17*	4	13
All commodities	*16**	*3*	*13*
Durable goods	16	0	16
Consumption goods	16*	4	12
Non-Am. farm products	16	5	11
Raw materials	16*	5	11
Capital equipment	14	0	14
Crop products, domestic	12*	2	10
Producer goods, all	10*	0	10
Metals	7	0	7
Producer goods for human consumption	7*	0	7

* Percentage of positive value changes at its minimum for the cycle.

Publications Still in Print
BOOKS

* Listed also as the first volume under Studies in Business Cycles.

TECHNICAL PAPERS

NATIONAL BUREAU OF ECONOMIC RESEARCH
1819 Broadway, New York 23, N. Y.